WORD OF THE DAY

WORD OF THE DAY

A SERIES TAILORED TO INSPIRE AND REINFORCE
YOUR DAILY LIFE

VOLUME 1

AIGBEFO D. EHIHI

Aishific
· p r e s s ·

Print ISBN: 979-8-8693-7315-1

Ebook ISBN: 979-8-8693-7316-8

Published by Aishific Press.

Aishific Press

www.aisific.com

books@aishific.com

1 (352) 300 6373

Printed in the United States of America.

Printed 2024.

CONTENTS

Dedication

To the One who speaks life into every word, this book is dedicated to our Lord and Savior, Jesus Christ, whose love, grace, and faithfulness inspire every step of this journey.

To my family, whose support and encouragement are a constant source of strength and joy—thank you for walking with me through every season.

And to you, dear reader, may these words bring light to your path, hope to your heart, and a deeper connection to the One who holds your every day.

This book is for you to inspire, encourage, and empower your journey, one word at a time.

With gratitude,

Dr. Aigbefo D. Ehihi

HOW TO USE THIS POWERFUL WORD OF THE DAY SERIES

Hi,

Welcome to the *Word of the Day* series! I am Dr. Aigbefo D. Ehihi, and I truly appreciate the opportunity to present this devotional to you today. This series is designed to inspire, encourage, and empower you with one carefully chosen word each day. Each word comes with scripture, reflection, and practical steps to help you grow spiritually, emotionally, and relationally. Whether you are beginning your day with it, pausing during a break, or reflecting in the evening, this series will provide you with daily moments of connection with God and His purpose for your life.

How It Works

- **One Word Per Day:** Each day centers on a single word, making it easy to focus, reflect, and apply.

- **Scripture for Context**: Each word is paired with a Bible verse to ground your reflection in God's Word.

- **Thought-Provoking Reflections**: The devotional includes reflections that explore the significance of the word and why it matters to your daily life.

- **Call-to-Action (CTA)**: Practical steps are included to encourage you to live out the lessons of the day.

- **Empowerment Through Prayer**: Prayer ties everything together, empowering you to walk boldly in faith.

Why This Matters

This series is more than just a devotional—it's an invitation to grow and reflect, one word at a time. It's an opportunity to slow down, tune into God's voice, and carry His truth into every part of your life.

By focusing on one word per day, you allow yourself to fully absorb its meaning and impact. The scriptures anchor your heart, the reflections challenge your thinking, and the practical actions inspire growth. It's a daily rhythm of empowerment and renewal.

Share the Journey

This *Word of the Day* series is perfect not just for you but also for friends, family, and loved ones. It's a thoughtful gift that encourages meaningful conversations and shared growth. By gifting this book to others, you can spark discussions around faith, life, and purpose as you journey through the words together.

Imagine the impact of sharing a daily word with a loved one, discussing its meaning, and holding each other accountable in living it out. Each word can uplift, challenge, and unite those who reflect on it together.

Get Your Copy and More

Grab a copy for yourself and consider gifting this series to friends and family. Share the journey of one word a day, and watch how it transforms your conversations, relationships, and faith.

Order your copy today and invite others to join you in this life-changing experience.

Together, let's grow, reflect, and live out God's purpose —one word at a time.

Thank you for allowing me to be part of your journey through this series. I pray it blesses and inspires you daily.

With gratitude,

Dr. Aigbefo D. Ehihi

1. TODAY'S WORD IS: HOPE

WEEK 1 DAY 1

Good morning!

Let's begin the day with a word that fuels the soul: **Hope**. Hope is the quiet assurance that there is light ahead no matter how dark today seems. It's the belief that better days are coming and the confidence that God's promises are unshakable.

A Thought to Reflect On:

In **Romans 15:13**, we find this powerful encouragement: *"May the God of hope fill you with all joy and peace as you trust in him, so that you may overflow with hope by the power of the Holy Spirit."* This verse reminds us that hope is not just an emotion—it's a gift from God that sustains us, bringing peace and joy even in uncertainty.

Why Does It Matter to You?: Hope is more than wishful thinking; it's a lifeline. When life feels overwhelming or uncertain, hope anchors you. It reminds you that setbacks are not permanent, and the challenges you face today shape you for a stronger tomorrow.

Without hope, it's easy to lose direction. With it, you gain clarity and strength to persevere. Hope transforms how you view your struggles—not as the end but as the beginning of something greater. It's the quiet voice that says, "Keep going," even when you feel like giving up.

Ask Yourself: What are you placing your hope in today? Is it in fleeting things or in the steadfast promises of God? Hope rooted in God is unshakable, providing peace in storms and courage in uncertainty.

Call-to-Action: Today, take one step to cultivate hope. It might be reading a scripture that uplifts your spirit, encouraging someone else, or taking a small action toward a dream you've put aside. Remember, even a glimmer of hope can light the path ahead.

📌 **Share this message with someone who could use a reminder of hope today, and let's spread this light together.**

Let hope lead you today and every day!

2. TODAY'S WORD IS: PURPOSE

WEEK 1 DAY 2

Good morning!

Let's set the tone for today with a powerful word: **Purpose**. Purpose is what gives life meaning and direction. It's the reason behind your actions and the driving force that helps you persevere through life's challenges.

A Thought to Reflect On:

In **Jeremiah 29:11**, God declares, *"For I know the plans I have for you, plans to prosper you and not to harm you, plans to give you hope and a future."* This verse reminds us that we are not here by accident. Each of us has been uniquely crafted with a purpose that aligns with God's greater plan.

Why Does It Matter to You?: Purpose shapes everything. Without it, life can feel aimless, like drifting without direction. But when you discover your purpose, even the most mundane tasks gain meaning. Purpose inspires you to get up each day with intention, knowing that what you do matters —not just to you but to others and God.

Purpose isn't about perfection; it's about progress. It's not always found in grand gestures or achievements. Often, it's discovered in how you treat others, the passion you pour into your work, or the love you bring to relationships.

Ask Yourself: *What's driving me today? Am I living intentionally or simply going through the motions?* When you align your actions with your purpose, you find fulfillment, strength, and clarity—even in the face of uncertainty.

Call-to-Action: Take a moment today to reconnect with your purpose. Reflect on one area of your life—your work, relationships, or spiritual journey—and ask, *How can I live with more intention?* Write down one action you'll take to align your efforts with what truly matters to you.

🖌 **Share this word with someone who inspires you to live with purpose, and let's encourage each other to walk intentionally.**

Live today with purpose, and let your actions reflect your calling!

3. TODAY'S WORD IS: FAITH

WEEK 1 DAY 3

Good morning!

Today's word is one that strengthens, sustains, and guides: **Faith**. Faith is the confidence in what we hope for and the assurance about what we do not see. It's the trust that God is working behind the scenes, even when life feels uncertain or unclear.

A Thought to Reflect On:

In **Hebrews 11:1**, we're reminded, *"Now faith is confidence in what we hope for and assurance about what we do not see."* This verse speaks to the power of faith—not as a blind leap, but as a firm trust in God's promises, even when the path forward isn't visible. Faith is the anchor that keeps us grounded when the waves of doubt threaten to overwhelm us.

Why Does It Matter to You?: Faith matters because it shifts your focus from what's uncertain to what's unchanging. Life is unpredictable, and circumstances will challenge your plans and beliefs. But faith gives you the strength to move forward, trusting that God is in control and has a plan for your life.

Faith doesn't eliminate challenges; it equips you to face them. It teaches you to rely not on your own strength but on the One who is all-powerful. Faith also fuels hope, reminding you that no matter how dark the night, the dawn is coming.

Ask Yourself: *Where is my faith rooted? Is it in fleeting things or in the eternal promises of God?* When your faith is firmly planted in God, you'll find peace that surpasses understanding and strength to overcome any obstacle.

Call-to-Action: Today, take a step to strengthen your faith. Whether it's through prayer, reading scripture, or simply pausing to reflect on God's goodness, choose an action that reaffirms your trust in Him. When doubt creeps in, remind yourself: *God is faithful, and He is for me.*

📌 **Share this word with someone who could use encouragement today, and let's build each other up in faith.**

**Let faith guide you today
—trust, believe, and move forward with confidence!**

4. TODAY'S WORD IS: GRACE

WEEK 1 DAY 4

Good morning!

Today's word is a gift that transforms lives: **Grace**. Grace is the unearned, unmerited favor of God. It's His kindness, love, and forgiveness freely given to us, not because we deserve it but because of who He is. Grace reminds us that we are deeply loved and valued even in our imperfections.

A Thought to Reflect On:

In **2 Corinthians 12:9**, God says, *"My grace is sufficient for you, for my power is made perfect in weakness."* This verse reassures us that grace isn't just about forgiveness—it's also the strength to carry on when we feel weak or unworthy. It's God's way of saying, *"You are enough because I am enough."*

Why Does It Matter to You?: Grace is life-changing because it frees you from the burden of trying to earn love or approval. It allows you to embrace your humanity, knowing that God's love covers your flaws and shortcomings. Grace isn't just for the big, life-altering moments; it's present in the every day—a kind word, a second chance, or the courage to try again.

Grace matters because it changes how we see ourselves and others. When you accept grace, you're empowered to extend it—to forgive those who've hurt you, to show kindness to someone struggling, or to give yourself the compassion you often withhold.

Ask Yourself: *Am I living in the freedom of grace, or am I weighed down by guilt and perfectionism? How can I extend grace to myself and those around me today?*

Call-to-Action: Take a moment today to rest in God's grace. Let go of something that's been weighing you down—a mistake, a regret, or a self-imposed expectation. Then, look for one way to extend grace to someone else. It could be offering forgiveness, a kind word, or a helping hand.

Share this message with someone who needs a reminder of God's grace, and let's spread His love through our actions.

> **Walk in grace today; let it transform**
> **how you see yourself and the world!**

5. TODAY'S WORD IS: STRENGTH

WEEK 1 DAY 5

Good morning!

Today's word is one that empowers and sustains: **Strength**. Strength is not just about physical power; it is the inner resilience, courage, and determination that help you rise above challenges. It's the assurance that with God, you are never alone in your struggles.

A Thought to Reflect On:

In **Philippians 4:13**, we're reminded, *"I can do all things through Christ who strengthens me."* This verse speaks to a strength that goes beyond human limits—a divine empowerment that enables you to endure, overcome, and thrive, no matter what life brings.

Why Does It Matter to You?: Strength matters because life often demands more of us than we think we can give. There are moments when challenges feel insurmountable, and you're tempted to give up. But strength isn't about having all the answers—it's about relying on God when you don't.

True strength is found in vulnerability, acknowledging your need for help, and trusting God to provide. It's the courage to take one more step when the road ahead feels uncertain. Strength isn't about never falling—it's about getting back up again and again and again.

Ask Yourself: *Where do I draw my strength from? Am I relying solely on my abilities, or am I leaning on God's power to sustain me?* When you choose to depend on Him, you'll discover a wellspring of strength that never runs dry.

Call-to-Action: Today, take a moment to draw on God's strength. Pray for His guidance in a situation that feels overwhelming. Then, take one small step forward, trusting that He will meet you there. Remember, His strength is made perfect in your weakness.

🔖 **Share this word with someone who may be struggling today, and remind them that strength comes from within and above.**

Let God's strength carry you today
—one step, one challenge, one victory at a time!

6. TODAY'S WORD IS: PERSEVERANCE

WEEK 1 DAY 6

Good morning!

Today's word is one that fuels progress and growth: **Perseverance**. Perseverance is the ability to stay committed and press forward, even when the road is hard, and the journey feels long. It's about choosing to keep going, trusting that your efforts are not in vain.

A Thought to Reflect On:

In **James 1:12**, we read, *"Blessed is the one who perseveres under trial because, having stood the test, that person will receive the crown of life that the Lord has promised to those who love him."* This verse reminds us that perseverance isn't just about endurance—it's about growing in faith and character, knowing that God has a reward waiting for us.

Why Does It Matter to You?: Perseverance matters because life is full of challenges that test your resolve. Whether it's a goal you are striving for, a relationship you are working to strengthen, or a trial you are enduring, perseverance helps you move forward, one step at a time.

It is easy to give up when progress feels too slow, or obstacles seem insurmountable, but perseverance teaches you patience and resilience. It reminds you that the most meaningful victories often come after the hardest battles. Perseverance is not just about grit—it is about trusting God to give you the strength to keep going, even when you feel weak. It is in Him we find the strength to persevere.

Ask Yourself: *Am I persevering in the areas that matter most? Am I trusting God to guide and sustain me, or am I trying to do it all on my own?* When you choose to persevere, you embrace the belief that your effort, guided by faith, will bear fruit in due time.

Call-to-Action: Today, commit to persevering in one area of your life where you have been tempted to give up. Take a small step forward—a prayer, an act of kindness, or a renewed effort toward a goal. Trust that God will meet you in your persistence and carry you through.

📌 **Share this word with someone who needs encouragement to keep going, and let's inspire each other to persevere.**

Persevere today, knowing that every step brings you closer to the blessings God has in store for you!

7. WEEKLY PAUSE: EMBRACING THE JOURNEY

WEEK 1 DAY 7

Good morning!

This week, we have explored powerful words that shape our lives—hope, purpose, faith, grace, strength, and perseverance. Each word challenges us to grow, trust, and move forward despite life's uncertainties. Take a moment to pause and consider how these truths have influenced your week.

Reflection

- Which word resonated most deeply with you this week?
- How has God been working in your life through these reflections?
- What challenges did you face, and how did these words equip you to overcome them?

Weekly Check-In

Let's celebrate progress:

- *What is one victory—big or small—that you experienced this week?*
- Renew your focus: *What is one area where you want to grow in the coming week?*

As you pause and reflect, remember that growth is not about perfection; it's about showing up with faith and perseverance, trusting that God is working in every moment.

Prayer

Heavenly Father, thank You for the lessons and blessings You have provided this week. Thank You for the hope that sustains us, the purpose that drives us, and the strength to keep moving forward. Lord, help us to walk in faith, extend grace to others, and persevere through challenges. As we step into a new week, may Your Spirit guide us, and may Your love fill our hearts. Helps us to always do the right at the right time. In Jesus' name, Amen.

8. TODAY'S WORD IS: LOVE

WEEK 2 DAY 1

Good morning!

Let's begin the day with a powerful word: **Love**. Love is at the heart of everything good and lasting. It is not just a feeling but a deliberate choice to care, give, and uplift others, reflecting God's love in our lives.

A Thought to Reflect On:

In **1 Corinthians 13:13**, we're reminded, *"And now these three remain: faith, hope, and love. But the greatest of these is love."* This verse reminds us that love is the highest virtue, surpassing all others. It's the foundation for how we live, connect, and serve.

Why Does It Matter to You?:

Love matters because it is the most profound way to reflect God's character. When you love others, you're not just showing kindness—you are embodying the essence of God's presence in your life. Love transforms relationships, heals wounds, and brings unity where there is division.

But love isn't always easy. It requires patience, forgiveness, and selflessness. It challenges you to love even when it's inconvenient or when others don't reciprocate. Yet, through love, you experience the fullness of God's joy and peace.

Ask Yourself: *How can I let God's love flow through me today? Am I holding back love because of fear, pride, or past hurt?* When you choose love, you choose freedom, healing, and connection.

Call-to-Action: Take one intentional step to show love today. Whether it's through a kind word, a thoughtful gesture, or a moment of forgiveness, let your actions reflect God's love. Remember, even small acts of love can have a profound impact.

Share this word with someone who inspires you to love deeply, and let's spread God's love together.

Let love be the foundation of all you do today—choose it, live it, share it.

9. TODAY'S WORD IS: GENTLENESS

WEEK 2 DAY 2

Good morning!

Today's word is **Gentleness**—a quiet strength that chooses kindness, compassion, and grace in every interaction. Gentleness is not weakness but power under control, reflecting God's love in how we treat others.

A Thought to Reflect On:

In **Philippians 4:5**, we're encouraged, *"Let your gentleness be evident to all. The Lord is near."* This verse reminds us that gentleness is a visible expression of our faith. It shows the world that God's presence in our lives brings peace and kindness, even in difficult moments.

Why Does It Matter to You?

Gentleness matters because it can transform relationships and situations. When faced with conflict or frustration, gentleness has the power to disarm anger, heal wounds, and create trust. It's a way of living that mirrors God's tender care for us.

In a world that often values assertiveness and dominance, gentleness reminds us that true strength lies in restraint and grace. It's easy to respond harshly when challenged, but gentleness chooses to listen, understand, and respond with love.

Ask Yourself: *Am I approaching others with gentleness, or am I letting frustration or pride dictate my actions? How can I reflect God's gentleness in my interactions today?*

Call-to-Action: Choose one moment today to practice gentleness—whether in your words, actions, or attitude. Let someone experience God's love through your compassion and kindness.

📌 **Share this word with someone who might need a reminder of the power of gentleness, and let's inspire one another to live with grace.**

Walk in gentleness today, and let it shape how you connect with others and God.

10. TODAY'S WORD IS: PATIENCE

WEEK 2 DAY 3

Good morning!

Today's word is **Patience**—the ability to endure delays, challenges, or discomfort without giving in to frustration. Patience is not passive; it's an active trust in God's perfect timing and plan.

A Thought to Reflect On:

In **Exodus 14:14**, we're reminded, *"The Lord will fight for you; you need only to be still."* This verse encourages us to embrace patience, trusting that God is at work even when we cannot see the full picture. Patience allows us to let go of control and lean into His faithfulness.

Why Does It Matter to You?

Patience is vital because life rarely unfolds according to our timeline. When we rush or resist the process, we often miss the lessons and blessings that come from waiting. Patience teaches us to persevere, to trust God's wisdom, and to respond with grace instead of haste.

Patience also deepens relationships, as it requires understanding and compassion. It reminds everyone, including you and I, that we are on our own journey. When you practice patience, you demonstrate strength, self-control, and faith in God's provision.

Ask Yourself: *Where in my life am I struggling to be patient? Am I trusting God's timing, or am I trying to force my own way?*

Call-to-Action: Pause before reacting today. Whether in a conversation, a frustrating moment, or an unanswered prayer, choose patience. Pray for God's peace to fill your heart and guide your actions.

📌 **Share this word with someone who needs encouragement to trust God's timing, and let's remind each other to embrace patience.**

Choose patience today
—trust the process, trust God, and let His timing bring peace to your heart.

11. TODAY'S WORD IS: HUMILITY

WEEK 2 DAY 4

Good morning!

Let's begin the day with a word that portrays our character: **Humility.** It is the ability to see ourselves honestly, recognize our dependence on God, and place the needs of others above our own. Humility isn't about thinking less of yourself but thinking of yourself less.

A Thought to Reflect On

In **Philippians 2:3**, we're instructed, *"Do nothing out of selfish ambition or vain conceit. Rather, in humility, value others above yourselves."* This verse challenges us to live with a spirit of service, letting humility guide our actions and relationships.

Why Does It Matter to You?

Humility matters because it fosters growth, connection, and harmony. It allows us to acknowledge our limitations and lean on God for strength and wisdom. In a world often driven by pride and self-promotion, humility shifts the focus from "me" to "we."

Humility also deepens relationships by opening the door to understanding and empathy. It teaches us to listen, to admit when we're wrong, and to lift others up instead of seeking our own recognition. When we practice humility, we reflect Christ's example of selfless love.

Ask Yourself: *Am I approaching life humbly, or am I allowing pride or self-interest to take the lead? How can I serve others today with a humble heart?*

Call-to-Action: Choose one act of humility today. It might be apologizing, letting someone else take the spotlight, or offering help without expecting anything in return. Let humility shape your actions and your attitude.

📌 **Share this word with someone who inspires you to live humbly, and let's encourage each other to follow Christ's example.**

Walk in humility today, and let it open your heart to God's grace and the needs of others.

12. TODAY'S WORD IS: FORGIVENESS

WEEK 2 DAY 5

Good morning!

Today's word is **Forgiveness**—the decision to release resentment and offer grace, just as God has done for us. Forgiveness doesn't erase the past but sets us free from its hold over our hearts.

A Thought to Reflect On

In **Ephesians 4:32**, we're reminded, *"Be kind and compassionate to one another, forgiving each other, just as in Christ God forgave you."* This verse encourages us to reflect on the immense forgiveness we've received from God and extend that same grace to others.

Why Does It Matter to You?

Forgiveness matters because it heals. Holding on to anger or bitterness doesn't hurt the person who wronged you—it hurts you. Forgiveness allows you to release the burden of pain, make space for peace, and move forward with a lighter heart.

Forgiveness also reflects God's character. When we forgive, we demonstrate His love and grace in action. It doesn't mean condoning the wrong, but it does mean choosing freedom over resentment.

Ask Yourself: *Is there someone I need to forgive today, or am I holding on to anger that's weighing me down? Have I forgiven myself for past mistakes?*

Call-to-Action: Take one step toward forgiveness today. It might be a prayer asking for the strength to forgive, writing a letter you never send, or having an honest conversation. Trust that God will give you the grace to let go and move forward.

Share this word with someone who may be struggling with forgiveness, and let's encourage each other to live in grace.

**Embrace forgiveness today
—it's a gift that sets both you and others free.**

13. TODAY'S WORD IS: PEACE

WEEK 2 DAY 6

Good morning!

Today's word is **Peace**—the calm assurance that God is in control, no matter the circumstances. Peace is not the absence of problems but the presence of God in the midst of them.

A Thought to Reflect On

In **John 14:27**, Jesus tells us, *"Peace I leave with you; my peace I give you. I do not give to you as the world gives. Do not let your hearts be troubled, and do not be afraid."* This verse reminds us that true peace doesn't come from external situations but from trusting God's promises and His presence in our lives.

Why Does It Matter to You?

Peace matters because life is often unpredictable and challenging. Anxiety, fear, and worry can steal your joy and cloud your perspective. But peace, rooted in faith, reminds you that you're not walking alone. God's peace guards your heart and mind, even when the world feels chaotic.

Peace also allows you to be a source of calm for others. When you carry God's peace, you can extend grace, patience, and understanding to those around you. It creates a ripple effect that touches hearts and transforms situations.

Ask Yourself: *Where in my life do I need God's peace today? Am I letting anxiety or fear take control, or am I trusting God to guide me?*

Call-to-Action: Take a moment today to pause and pray for peace in your heart. Identify one worry or fear and give it to God. Let His peace replace your anxiety. Then, share that peace by offering encouragement or kindness to someone else.

Share this word with someone who may be seeking peace today, and let's spread God's calm assurance together.

Let God's peace fill your heart today, and may it guide you in all you do.

14. WEEKLY PAUSE: REFLECTING ON LOVE, GRACE, AND PEACE

WEEK 2 DAY 7

Good Morning,

This week, we explored the transformative power of love, gentleness, patience, humility, forgiveness, and peace. These words remind us of God's character and how we are called to reflect His love in our actions and relationships. Let's take this moment to pause and reflect on how these virtues have shaped our hearts and lives this week.

Reflection

- Which word resonated most deeply with you this week, and why?
- How did practicing these virtues impact your relationships, attitude, or perspective?
- In what ways did you experience God's presence as you embraced these truths?

Weekly Check-In

- Celebrate progress: *What small victories or changes are you proud of this week?*
- Renew your focus: *What is one area where you can continue to grow in the coming week?*

Remember, growth happens step by step, and God's grace is with you every step of the way.

Prayer

Heavenly Father, thank You for Your love, which guides and sustains us. Thank You for teaching us to live with gentleness, patience, and humility and for showing us the freedom found in forgiveness and peace. Lord, as we step into a new week, help us carry these lessons in our hearts. Let our actions reflect Your love and bring hope to those around us. We trust in Your peace and grace to lead us forward. In Jesus' name, Amen.

Take this week's lessons into your heart, and let God's love guide your journey forward!

15. TODAY'S WORD IS: COURAGE

WEEK 3 DAY 1

Good morning!

Let's begin the day with a word that fuels boldness and action: **Courage**. Courage is the strength to face challenges, take risks, and trust in God's promises, even when fear tries to hold you back. It's not about the absence of fear but about stepping forward in faith despite it.

A Thought to Reflect On

In **Joshua 1:9**, we're reminded, *"Be strong and courageous. Do not be afraid; do not be discouraged, for the Lord your God will be with you wherever you go."* This verse reassures us that our courage is rooted in God's unwavering presence. His strength enables us to face any obstacle with confidence.

Why Does It Matter to You?

Courage matters because fear often tries to limit us. It whispers doubts, highlights risks, and creates hesitation when

God calls us to move. Courage breaks through those barriers, reminding us that God's power is greater than our fears.

It's not just for life's monumental moments; courage is required in the every day—in making difficult choices, standing up for what's right, or trusting God's plan when the future is unclear. Courage inspires action and aligns us with God's purposes.

Ask Yourself: *Where in my life do I need courage today? What fear or hesitation can I surrender to God?*

Call-to-Action: Take one courageous step today. It could be as simple as speaking up, making a bold decision, or trusting God with a situation you've been holding back on. Remember, He is with you every step of the way.

Share this word with someone who inspires you to live boldly, and let's build courage together.

Step forward with courage today—God is with you, and His strength will guide your path!

16. TODAY'S WORD IS: SELF-CONTROL

Good morning!

Let's start the day with a word that empowers us to align our actions with God's will: **Self-Control**. Self-control is the ability to master our emotions, desires, and impulses, allowing us to make choices that reflect God's wisdom rather than fleeting feelings.

A Thought to Reflect On

In **Proverbs 25:28**, we're reminded, *"Like a city whose walls are broken through is a person who lacks self-control."* This passage paints a vivid picture of how self-control protects and strengthens us, just as sturdy walls protect a city. Without it, we're vulnerable to chaos and poor decisions.

Why Does It Matter to You?

Self-control matters because it gives us the power to live with intention. Instead of being driven by anger, impatience, or temptation, self-control allows us to pause, reflect, and respond in ways that honor God and benefit others.

In a world that often promotes instant gratification, self-control helps us prioritize what's lasting over what's immediate. It's not about perfection—it's about progress and surrendering to God's guidance each day.

Ask Yourself: *Are there areas of my life where I've been letting emotions or impulses take control? How can I practice self-control to reflect God's will today?*

Call-to-Action: Choose one moment today to practice self-control. It might be holding your tongue when tempted to speak harshly, saying no to temptation, or making time for prayer instead of distractions. Let your actions be a reflection of God's presence in your life.

Share this word with someone who might need encouragement to live with intention, and let's inspire each other to grow in self-control.

Embrace self-control today—trusting that God will strengthen and guide you in every decision.

17. TODAY'S WORD IS: ATTITUDE

WEEK 3 DAY 3

Good morning!

Let's begin the day with a word that shapes how we experience life: **Attitude**. Your attitude is a reflection of your heart and mindset. A Christ-centered attitude radiates gratitude, faith, and joy, even in the midst of challenges.

A Thought to Reflect On

In **Philippians 2:14-15**, we're reminded, *"Do everything without grumbling or arguing, so that you may become blameless and pure, children of God without fault in a warped and crooked generation."* This verse challenges us to cultivate an attitude of humility and positivity, reflecting God's light in all we do.

Why Does It Matter to You?

Attitude matters because it influences your perspective and your impact on others. When you approach life with gratitude and faith, you invite God's peace into your heart and inspire those around you. On the other hand, negativity and complaining can cloud your judgment and hinder your spiritual growth.

Your attitude is a choice. While you can't always control your circumstances, you can control how you respond to them. A Christlike attitude transforms challenges into opportunities for growth and shows others the hope and joy that come from trusting God.

Ask Yourself: *Is my attitude reflecting faith and gratitude today? How can I shift my perspective to better align with God's truth?*

Call-to-Action: Choose to cultivate a positive attitude today. When frustration or negativity arises, pause and pray for God's perspective. Speak words of encouragement to yourself and those around you, letting your attitude reflect God's love.

Share this word with someone who brings light into your life, and let's encourage one another to live with joyful hearts.

Let your attitude reflect Christ today—choose gratitude, joy, and faith in every moment!

18. TODAY'S WORD IS: FAITHFULNESS

WEEK 3 DAY 4

Good morning!

Let's begin the day with a word that reflects God's character: **Faithfulness**. Faithfulness is steadfastness, reliability, and commitment. It means staying true to God, His promises, and the responsibilities He's entrusted to you.

A Thought to Reflect On

In **1 Corinthians 4:2**, we're reminded, *"Now it is required that those who have been given a trust must prove faithful."* This verse challenges us to honor the trust God has placed in us by living with integrity and consistency in every aspect of our lives.

Why Does It Matter to You?

Faithfulness matters because it builds trust and strengthens relationships. It's a daily choice to keep your commitments, show up for others, and remain anchored in God's truth, even when life feels uncertain or challenging.

Faithfulness also reflects God's unwavering love for us. Just as He is faithful to His promises, we're called to reflect that faithfulness in how we live, love, and serve. It's not about perfection but perseverance—choosing to stay the course, no matter how difficult.

Ask Yourself: *Am I being faithful to God's calling, to my commitments, and to the people in my life? Where can I grow in faithfulness today?*

Call-to-Action: Take one step today to practice faithfulness. It could be honoring a promise, following through on a task, or spending intentional time with God. Let your actions reflect the steadfast love of the One who is always faithful.

Share this word with someone who inspires you to live with integrity, and let's encourage each other to remain faithful.

Walk in faithfulness today—stay committed, stay steadfast, and trust God's unchanging promises!

19. TODAY'S WORD IS: AWARENESS
WEEK 3 DAY 5

Good morning!

Let's begin the day with a word that invites us to live fully present: **Awareness.** Awareness is the ability to recognize God's presence, understand your emotions, and notice the needs of others. It's about being mindful of what truly matters.

A Thought to Reflect On:

In **Psalm 139:23-24**, we read, *"Search me, God, and know my heart; test me and know my anxious thoughts. See if there is any offensive way in me, and lead me in the way everlasting."* This passage reminds us that awareness begins with inviting God to reveal what's in our hearts and guide us toward His truth.

Why Does It Matter to You?

Awareness matters because it's easy to get caught up in distractions, routines, or emotions that cloud your perspective. When you're aware—of God's presence, your own thoughts, and the needs of others—you're able to make intentional, faith-driven choices.

Self-awareness allows you to grow spiritually by recognizing areas where you need God's grace. Awareness of others helps you extend compassion and support. And awareness of God keeps you anchored in His love and guidance.

Ask Yourself: *Am I fully present in my life, or am I distracted by worries or busyness? How can I cultivate greater awareness of God, myself, and others today?*

Call-to-Action: Take a moment today to pause and reflect. Spend time in prayer or stillness, asking God to heighten your awareness. Notice one area of your life where you've been distracted, and commit to giving it your full attention with God's help.

📌 **Share this word with someone who inspires you to live mindfully, and let's encourage each other to grow in awareness.**

Live with awareness today—stay present, seek God's guidance, and embrace the moments that matter most.

20. TODAY'S WORD IS: WATCHFULNESS

WEEK 3 DAY 6

Good morning!

Let's begin the day with a word that calls us to stay spiritually alert: **Watchfulness**. Watchfulness is the ability to remain vigilant and attentive to God's direction, ready to act boldly in faith when opportunities or challenges arise.

A Thought to Reflect On

In **1 Corinthians 16:13**, we're encouraged, *"Be on your guard; stand firm in the faith; be courageous; be strong."* This verse reminds us that watchfulness is about being spiritually prepared—staying grounded in faith and ready to respond to God's calling.

Why Does It Matter to You?

Watchfulness matters because life is full of distractions that can pull your attention away from what truly matters. When you're watchful, you can discern God's guidance, recognize His work in your life, and respond with boldness and trust.

Watchfulness also protects you from spiritual complacency. It keeps your faith active, your heart open, and your mind focused on God's purpose for your life. Being watchful allows you to act courageously and clearly when God calls you to move.

Ask Yourself: *Am I staying alert physically, spiritually, and emotionally? What distractions have been causing me to lose my focus lately? How can I be watchful for God's direction today?*

Call-to-Action: Take time today to pause and pray for spiritual clarity. Ask God to help you remain watchful for His guidance and prepared to act boldly when needed. Stay mindful of His presence and purpose in every moment.

Share this word with someone who inspires you to stay strong in faith, and let's encourage one another to live watchfully.

**Be watchful today—stand firm in faith,
trust God's timing, and act boldly when He calls.**

21. WEEKLY PAUSE: CULTIVATING INNER STRENGTH AND FAITH

WEEK 3 DAY 7

Good morning!

This week, we reflected on courage, self-control, attitude, faithfulness, awareness, and watchfulness. These words remind us of the inner strength and focus needed to live a life rooted in God's purpose. Let's take this moment to reflect on how these virtues have deepened our faith and shaped our actions.

Reflection

- Which word resonated most deeply with you this week?
- How did practicing these virtues help you grow in your relationship with God?
- What challenges did you face, and how did God's guidance help you overcome them?

Check-In

- Celebrate progress: *What small victories or moments of growth are you celebrating this week?*
- Renew focus: *Where do you feel called to strengthen your inner resilience or trust in God in the coming week?*

Remember, cultivating these virtues is a lifelong journey, and God's grace is with you every step of the way.

Prayer

Heavenly Father, thank You for the lessons You've taught us this week. Thank You for giving us the courage to face fears, the self-control to align our actions with Your will, and the faithfulness to stay true to Your purpose. Lord, help us remain watchful, aware of Your presence, and steadfast in our attitude and trust. As we enter a new week, guide us to walk boldly in Your truth and reflect Your love in all we do. In Jesus' name, Amen.

Let this week's lessons strengthen your heart and inspire your journey forward in faith!

22. TODAY'S WORD IS: CONFIDENCE

WEEK 4 DAY 1

Good morning!

L et's begin the day with a word that inspires boldness and trust: **Confidence**. Confidence is not about relying on your own abilities but trusting in God's promises and stepping forward in faith, knowing He is with you every step of the way.

A Thought to Reflect On

In **Hebrews 13:6**, we're reminded, *"So we say with confidence, 'The Lord is my helper; I will not be afraid.'"* This verse reassures us that true confidence comes from knowing we are not alone. God's strength, guidance, and presence give us the courage to face any challenge or uncertainty.

Why Does It Matter to You?

Confidence matters because fear and doubt often try to hold us back from fulfilling God's purpose for our lives. When we focus on our own limitations, it's easy to feel overwhelmed or unworthy. But confidence rooted in God reminds us that His power works through our weaknesses.

Confidence also equips us to take action. It helps us step out of our comfort zones, pursue God-given opportunities, and trust His plan even when the path is unclear. It's a reflection of faith that says, *"I trust You, Lord, to lead me where I need to go."*

Ask Yourself: *Where in my life do I need to let go of fear and embrace God's confidence? How can I trust Him more today?*

Call-to-Action: Take one bold step today that reflects your confidence in God. It could be starting something you've been afraid to try, offering encouragement to someone, or simply trusting His timing in a situation you've been anxious about.

Share this word with someone who needs encouragement to live boldly, and let's build each other up in faith and confidence.

Walk in confidence today—trusting that God is with you, guiding and strengthening you in all you do.

23. TODAY'S WORD IS: DISCIPLINE

WEEK 4 DAY 2

Good morning!

Let's begin the day with a word that empowers growth and purpose: **Discipline**. Discipline is the practice of aligning your actions, habits, and choices with God's will, even when it requires sacrifice or perseverance.

A Thought to Reflect On

In **Hebrews 12:11**, we're reminded, *"No discipline seems pleasant at the time, but painful. Later on, however, it produces a harvest of righteousness and peace for those who have been trained by it."* This verse reminds us that discipline may be challenging in the moment, but it brings lasting growth, peace, and alignment with God's purpose for our lives.

Why Does It Matter to You?

Discipline matters because it helps us stay focused on what truly matters. Without discipline, we're more likely to give in to distractions, laziness, or instant gratification. Discipline keeps us rooted in God's truth, guiding our decisions and strengthening our faith.

It also equips us to persevere through challenges. Discipline reminds us to stay the course, even when it's hard, trusting that God's plan is worth the effort. It's an act of faith and obedience that brings us closer to His will.

Ask Yourself: *Where in my life do I need greater discipline? Are there areas where I've been prioritizing comfort over growth or purpose?*

Call-to-Action: Identify one area today where you can practice discipline. It could be setting aside time for prayer, resisting temptation, or committing to a task you've been avoiding. Trust that the effort you make now will yield a harvest of peace and righteousness.

📌 **Share this word with someone who inspires you to stay disciplined in faith, and let's encourage each other to keep growing.**

Embrace discipline today—let it strengthen your faith, guide your actions, and draw you closer to God.

24. TODAY'S WORD IS: SELFLESSNESS

WEEK 4 DAY 3

Good morning!

Let's begin the day with a word that reflects Christ's heart: **Selflessness**. Selflessness is the act of putting others' needs above your own, showing love and humility in a way that mirrors God's grace toward us.

A Thought to Reflect On

In **Philippians 2:3**, we're reminded, *"Do nothing out of selfish ambition or vain conceit. Rather, in humility, value others above yourselves."* This verse calls us to live with a heart of humility, focusing on the well-being of others rather than seeking recognition or personal gain.

Why Does It Matter to You?

Selflessness matters because it shifts our perspective from "me" to "we." In a world often centered on self-promotion, selflessness challenges us to reflect God's love by serving others with humility and compassion.

Selflessness also deepens relationships. It creates an environment of trust and care where others feel valued and supported. When we act selflessly, we honor God's call to love one another and experience the joy that comes from giving without expecting anything in return.

Ask Yourself: *How can I show selflessness in my actions today? Are there areas where I've been focusing too much on myself instead of others?*

Call-to-Action: Choose one act of selflessness today. It could be helping someone in need, offering your time or resources, or simply being fully present for a loved one. Let your actions reflect Christ's love and humility.

📌 **Share this word with someone who inspires you to live selflessly, and let's encourage each other to serve with love.**

Practice selflessness today—put others first, and let your actions reflect God's heart.

25. TODAY'S WORD IS: KINDNESS

WEEK 4 DAY 4

Good morning!

Let's begin the day with a word that embodies God's love in action: **Kindness**. Kindness is the simple yet profound act of showing compassion, care, and understanding toward others, reflecting God's grace in every interaction.

A Thought to Reflect On

In **Ephesians 4:32**, we're reminded, *"Be kind and compassionate to one another, forgiving each other, just as in Christ God forgave you."* This verse encourages us to embody kindness in how we treat others, letting forgiveness and love guide our actions.

Why Does It Matter to You?

Kindness matters because it has the power to heal, uplift, and strengthen relationships. A kind word or gesture can brighten someone's day, mend a broken heart, or inspire hope in a difficult situation.

Kindness also reflects God's character. When we act kindly, we demonstrate His love to those around us. It's not always easy—especially when others are difficult—but choosing kindness is a powerful way to honor God and build meaningful connections.

Ask Yourself: *How can I show kindness today? Are there moments when I've missed opportunities to reflect God's love through my actions?*

Call-to-Action: Look for an opportunity to show kindness today. It could be as simple as a smile, a word of encouragement, or helping someone in need. Let your actions be a reflection of God's compassion and grace.

Share this word with someone who inspires you to live kindly, and let's encourage one another to spread God's love.

Choose kindness today—be a light in someone's life and reflect the heart of God.

26. TODAY'S WORD IS: SERVICE

WEEK 4 DAY 5

Good morning!

Let's begin the day with a word that calls us to action: **Service**. Service is humbly using your gifts and time to bless others and glorify God. It reflects Christ's love, shown through acts of compassion and generosity.

A Thought to Reflect On:

In **1 Peter 4:10**, we're reminded, *"Each of you should use whatever gift you have received to serve others as faithful stewards of God's grace in its various forms."* This passage reminds us that service is a duty and a privilege—an opportunity to share God's grace and love.

Why Does It Matter to You?

Service matters because it shifts our focus from ourselves to others. It's an act of worship that demonstrates love, humility, and obedience to God's calling. Service also brings joy and purpose as we see how our actions can make a difference in someone else's life.

When we serve, we reflect Christ's example. His life was one of selfless service, showing us that greatness comes not from being served but from serving others. Whether through small gestures or significant sacrifices, service is a powerful way to live out our faith.

Ask Yourself: *How can I serve others today? Are there opportunities to use my gifts and time to glorify God and bless those around me?*

Call-to-Action: Identify one way to serve today—whether through helping someone in need, volunteering your time, or offering encouragement. Let your service be a reflection of God's love and grace.

Share this word with someone who inspires you to serve, and let's encourage each other to live with purpose and compassion.

Serve with humility and joy today—using your gifts to glorify God and bless others.

27. TODAY'S WORD IS: GENEROSITY

WEEK 4 DAY 6

Good morning!

Let's begin the day with a word that reflects the abundance of God's love: **Generosity**. Generosity is the act of giving freely—of your time, resources, or kindness —without expecting anything in return. It's a tangible expression of God's grace and provision in your life.

A Thought to Reflect On

In **Proverbs 11:25**, we're reminded, *"A generous person will prosper; whoever refreshes others will be refreshed."* This verse highlights the reciprocal blessing of generosity: as we pour into others, God pours back into us, enriching our lives in ways we cannot measure.

Why Does It Matter to You?

Generosity matters because it aligns our hearts with God's. When we give freely, we reflect His abundant love and provision in our lives. Generosity shifts our focus from scarcity to abundance, reminding us that God provides for our needs so that we can bless others.

Generosity also builds community and trust. It creates opportunities to share God's love in practical ways, touching hearts and inspiring faith. Whether through financial giving, acts of kindness, or sharing your time, generosity transforms both the giver and the receiver.

Ask Yourself: *Where in my life can I practice generosity today? How can I reflect God's love by giving freely to others?*

Call-to-Action: Choose one way to practice generosity today. It could be as simple as sharing encouragement, helping someone in need, or giving to a cause that reflects God's heart. Let your actions remind others of God's abundant love.

🕊 **Share this word with someone who inspires you to give generously, and let's encourage each other to be vessels of God's grace.**

Embrace generosity today—give freely, love abundantly, and reflect God's heart in all you do.

28. WEEKLY PAUSE: SERVING WITH DISCIPLINE AND CONFIDENCE

WEEK 4 DAY 7

Good morning!

This week, we reflected on confidence, discipline, selflessness, kindness, service, and generosity. These words remind us how our actions can reflect God's love, calling us to live with purpose and compassion. Let's take this moment to pause and consider how these virtues have shaped our week.

Reflection

- Which word spoke to you most deeply this week?
- How did practicing these virtues impact your relationship with God and others?
- What challenges did you face, and how did God's strength guide you through them?
- How do you plan to implement this word?

Check-In

- *What small victories or steps of growth are you celebrating this week?*
- *In what ways do you feel God is calling you to continue growing in confidence, discipline, and service?*

Prayer

Lord, thank You for teaching us to walk confidently in Your promises and embrace discipline daily. Thank You for showing us the beauty of selflessness, kindness, service, and generosity and for reminding us that every act of love reflects Your heart. As we step into a new week, guide us to continue serving with discipline and confidence, bringing glory to Your name. In Jesus' name, Amen.

Carry these lessons forward into the next week, trusting God's guidance in all you do!

29. TODAY'S WORD IS: WISDOM

WEEK 5 DAY 1

Good morning!

Let's begin the day with a word that brings clarity and guidance: **Wisdom**. Wisdom is more than knowledge —it's the ability to discern and apply God's truth in your life, making decisions that honor Him and lead to growth.

A Thought to Reflect On

In **Proverbs 9:10**, we're reminded, *"The fear of the Lord is the beginning of wisdom, and knowledge of the Holy One is understanding."* This verse teaches us that true wisdom starts with reverence for God. When we seek Him first, His guidance shapes our decisions and illuminates our path.

Why Does It Matter to You?

Wisdom matters because life is full of choices, and not every option is aligned with God's purpose. Wisdom equips you to navigate challenges, avoid pitfalls, and pursue what is good and right. It helps you discern between fleeting desires and lasting values.

Wisdom also deepens your relationship with God and others. It teaches you to listen more than speak, to consider consequences before acting, and to prioritize what truly matters. Through wisdom, you reflect God's truth and grace in your life.

Ask Yourself: *Am I seeking God's wisdom in my daily decisions? How can I prioritize His guidance over my own understanding today?*

Call-to-Action: Spend time in prayer or scripture today, asking God for wisdom in one specific area of your life. Let His Word guide your decisions and clarify any uncertainties you face.

Share this word with someone who inspires you to seek God's wisdom, and let's encourage each other to live wisely.

Seek wisdom today—let God's truth guide your choices and lead you closer to His purpose.

30. TODAY'S WORD IS: INTEGRITY

WEEK 5 DAY 2

Good morning!

Let's begin the day with a word that reflects steadfast character: **Integrity**. Integrity is living with honesty, consistency, and faithfulness to God's truth, even when no one else is watching.

A Thought to Reflect On:

Proverbs 11:3 reminds us that *"the integrity of the upright leads them, but the unfaithful are ruined by their deceit."* This verse emphasizes that integrity serves as a reliable guide, directing us toward righteousness and protecting us from the dangers of dishonesty.

Why Does It Matter to You?

Integrity matters because it builds trust—with God, with others, and within yourself. Living with integrity means aligning your actions with your beliefs, ensuring that your words and deeds reflect God's truth.

It also strengthens your witness to others. Integrity shows the world that your faith isn't just something you profess and live out daily. It creates consistency in your relationships and a sense of peace, knowing that you are honoring God with your life.

Ask Yourself: *Are my actions and words aligned with God's truth? Do others see me as a person of integrity? How can I live with greater integrity today?*

Call-to-Action: Choose one way to practice integrity today. Whether it's being honest in a tough situation, following through on a promise, or standing firm in your faith, let your actions reflect God's truth and love.

Share this word with someone who inspires you to live with integrity, and let's encourage each other to remain faithful to God's guidance.

Live with integrity today—honor God by aligning your actions with His truth.

31. TODAY'S WORD IS: FIDELITY

WEEK 5 DAY 3

Good morning!

Let's begin the day with a word that speaks to faithfulness and loyalty: **Fidelity**. Fidelity is staying true to your commitments, responsibilities, and relationships, reflecting God's unwavering faithfulness to us.

A Thought to Reflect On

In **Proverbs 28:20**, we're reminded, *"A faithful person will be richly blessed, but one eager to get rich will not go unpunished."* This verse highlights the blessings that come from living with fidelity—remaining steadfast in your responsibilities and faithful to God's calling.

Why Does It Matter to You?

Fidelity matters because it builds trust, strengthens relationships, and honors God. It's not just about keeping promises

—it's about living with integrity, dedication, and consistency in every area of life.

In a world that often values convenience over commitment, fidelity stands out as a reflection of God's character. Just as He is faithful to His promises, we are called to reflect that faithfulness in how we approach our work, relationships, and faith journey.

Ask Yourself: *Am I staying faithful to my commitments? Where can I grow in fidelity to God and those around me? Am I faithful to my spouse, friends, or loved ones?*

Call-to-Action: Take a moment today to reflect on your commitments and responsibilities. Choose one area where you can show greater fidelity—whether it's following through on a promise, deepening a relationship, or staying steadfast in prayer.

📌 **Share this word with someone who inspires you to stay faithful, and let's encourage each other to live with fidelity.**

Walk in fidelity today—stay true to your word, responsibilities, and faith in God.

32. TODAY'S WORD IS: TRUST
WEEK 5 DAY 4

Good morning!

Let's begin the day with a word that invites surrender and peace: **Trust**. Trust is placing your confidence in God's promises and His plan, even when the path ahead is unclear.

A Thought to Reflect On

In **Proverbs 3:5**, we're reminded, *"Trust in the Lord with all your heart and lean not on your own understanding."* This verse encourages us to let go of control and rely on God's wisdom and faithfulness, knowing He is always working for our good.

Why Does It Matter to You?

Trust matters because life is full of uncertainties. It's easy to feel anxious or overwhelmed when things don't go as planned. Trusting God allows you to release those burdens and rest in the assurance that He is in control.

Trust also deepens your relationship with God. It reminds you to seek His guidance, rely on His strength, and believe in His promises, even when you don't see immediate results. Trust is a daily choice to walk by faith, not by sight.

Ask Yourself: *Where am I struggling to trust God today? How can I surrender my fears and lean on His promises?*

Call-to-Action: Take one step of trust today. Whether it's through prayer, letting go of a worry, or choosing faith over fear, allow God to guide you. Trust that He is working all things for your good

Share this word with someone who inspires you to trust God, and let's encourage each other to walk in faith.

Choose trust today—release your worries and rest in the peace of God's promises.

33. TODAY'S WORD IS: HONOR

Good morning!

Let's begin the day with a word that elevates our relationships and actions: **Honor**. Honor is showing respect, reverence, and value toward God and others. It's a way of living that reflects the worth God has placed in each person.

A Thought to Reflect On

In **Romans 12:10**, we're reminded, *"Be devoted to one another in love. Honor one another above yourselves."* This verse calls us to treat others with love and respect, placing their needs and dignity above ours.

Why Does It Matter to You?

Honor matters because it reflects God's heart. When you choose to honor others—your family, friends, coworkers, or even strangers—you acknowledge their worth as creations of God. Honor builds trust, strengthens relationships, and fosters peace.

Honoring God means aligning your life with His will and giving Him the highest place in your heart. It's about living in obedience, gratitude, and reverence for His holiness. Honor is not just about words but about actions reflecting love and respect.

Ask Yourself: *Am I honoring God with my life? How can I show greater honor to those around me today?*

Call-to-Action: Choose one act of honor today. It could be as simple as showing appreciation, listening attentively, or serving someone selflessly. Let your actions reflect the love and respect God calls us to show.

🖈 **Share this word with someone who inspires you to live honorably, and let's encourage each other to reflect God's heart.**

Live with honor today—elevate God in your heart and value the people He has placed in your life.

34. TODAY'S WORD IS: RESPECT

WEEK 5 DAY 6

Good morning!

Let's begin the day with a word that strengthens our connections with others: **Respect**. Respect is valuing and treating others with dignity, as every person is created in God's image and reflects His handiwork.

A Thought to Reflect On

In **Matthew 7:12**, we're reminded, *"So in everything, do to others what you would have them do to you, for this sums up the Law and the Prophets."* This verse calls us to treat others with kindness and fairness, embodying the love and respect God shows to us.

Why Does It Matter to You?

Respect matters because it builds trust and harmony in relationships. When you treat others respectfully, you reflect God's love and acknowledge their worth as His creation.

Respect goes beyond words—it's shown through actions, listening, and honoring others' feelings and perspectives.

Respect also fosters humility and compassion. It reminds us to value people not for what they can do for us but for who they are in God's eyes. When we respect others, we cultivate peace and understanding, creating an environment where God's love can thrive.

Ask Yourself: *Am I showing respect to those around me? Are there ways I can better honor the people God has placed in my life?*

Call-to-Action: Show respect in a meaningful way today. Listen without interrupting, offer encouragement, or take time to recognize someone's contributions or feelings. Let your actions reflect the dignity God places on every life.

Share this word with someone who inspires you to live respectfully, and let's encourage each other to build relationships rooted in God's love.

Choose respect today—honor others as God honors you, and let His love shine through your actions.

35. WEEKLY PAUSE: LIVING WITH WISDOM AND HONOR

WEEK 5 DAY 7

Good morning!

This week, we reflected on wisdom, integrity, fidelity, trust, honor, and respect. These words remind us of the foundation of a Christ-centered life—aligning our hearts and actions with God's truth while valuing others as He does. Let's take this moment to reflect on how these virtues have shaped our hearts and lives this week. As you reflect, think about what these words mean to you.

Reflection

- Which word resonated most deeply with you this week?
- How did practicing these virtues influence your decisions, relationships, or connection with God?
- What challenges did you face, and how did these words guide you in overcoming them?

Check-In

- *What small victories are you celebrating this week?*
- *In what areas is God calling you to deepen your walk in wisdom, honor, or trust?*

Remember, these virtues are not destinations but ongoing journeys. God's grace equips us to live them out daily.

Prayer

Heavenly Father, thank You for the wisdom You provide, the integrity You inspire, and the faithfulness You show us daily. Thank You for teaching us trust, honor, and respect as we seek to reflect Your love in all we do. Lord, as we move into a new week, help us to live with purpose and humility, walking boldly in Your truth and grace. In Jesus' name, Amen.

Let these words guide your actions and encourage your heart as you step into the new week with purpose and faith!

36. TODAY'S WORD IS: OBEDIENCE

WEEK 6 DAY 1

Good morning!

Let's begin the day with a word that calls us to align our actions and hearts with God's will: **Obedience**. Obedience is more than just following rules—it's an expression of trust in God's wisdom and a reflection of our desire to honor Him in all that we do.

A Thought to Reflect On

In **1 Samuel 15:22**, God reminds us, *"To obey is better than sacrifice, and to heed is better than the fat of rams."* These words highlight that God values our obedience above all else, even more than any offering or external acts of worship. Obedience is an act of surrender; it involves yielding our personal aspirations and desires to align ourselves with God's greater purpose and divine plan. This act of submission reflects our trust in His wisdom and signifies a willingness to embrace a path that may surpass our understanding.

Why Does It Matter to You?

Obedience isn't just about following instructions; it's about aligning your heart with God's purpose for your life. When we obey, we invite God's will to guide our decisions, shape our character, and deepen our relationship with Him. Complete obedience requires trust—trust that God knows what is best for us, even when His plan doesn't make sense or challenges us.

Ask Yourself: *What areas in my life is God calling me to be completely obedient?* It could be something simple like being more patient with others or surrendering a specific area of your life. What will it cost you to fully obey, whether God or Authority figures?

Call-to-Action: Today, focus on obeying God in small ways. Whether it's showing kindness when you would rather not, following through on a commitment, trusting God with an uncertain future, or just living righteously. Choose to obey and see how He blesses your obedience.

📌 **Obey today, and experience the joy that comes from trusting God fully.**

Let's choose obedience over sacrifice and watch how God works through our willingness to follow His lead.

37. TODAY'S WORD IS: SUBMISSION

Good morning!

Let's begin the day with a word that reminds us to surrender our plans to God's greater purpose: **Submission**. Submission is not about weakness; it's about humbling ourselves before God and trusting His will above our own.

A Thought to Reflect On

In **James 4:7**, we're instructed, *"Submit yourselves, then, to God. Resist the devil, and he will flee from you."* This verse reminds us that submission to God is the key to spiritual strength. When we submit ourselves to Him, we open our hearts to His guidance and protection, thereby enabling His power to work within and through us. This act of submission plays a crucial role in facilitating the process of humility.

Why Does It Matter to You?

Submission matters because it frees us from the burden of trying to control everything. It's easy to hold tightly to our own plans, but true freedom comes when we trust God to lead us. Submission is an act of faith, acknowledging that His ways are higher and His plans are better.

When we submit to God, we grow in humility, trust, and dependence on Him. It allows us to resist temptations, overcome fears, and walk boldly in His purpose.

Ask Yourself: *What areas of my life am I holding onto too tightly? How can I submit them to God today? Where in my life needs more submission?*

Call-to-Action: Take one step today to practice submission. Whether it's surrendering a worry, giving up control over a situation, or seeking God's will in prayer, choose to let go and trust Him fully.

📌 **Share this word with someone who inspires you to live in surrender to God, and let's encourage each other to walk in submission.**

Submit to God today—release control, trust His plan, and experience the peace that comes from surrendering to His will.

38. TODAY'S WORD IS: REVERENCE

WEEK 6 DAY 3

Good morning!

Let's begin the day with a word that calls us to honor and stand in awe of God: **Reverence**. Reverence is a deep respect for God's holiness, power, and love—a response of worship and humility before the Creator of all.

A Thought to Reflect On

In **Hebrews 12:28**, we're reminded, *"Let us be thankful, and so worship God acceptably with reverence and awe."* This verse encourages us to approach God with gratitude and a profound sense of His greatness, acknowledging His sovereignty and majesty.

Why Does It Matter to You?

Reverence matters because it shapes how we approach God and live our lives. When we live with reverence, we're reminded of God's holiness and our need for His grace. It leads us to worship humbly, pray sincerely, and serve with a heart aligned to His will.

Reverence also deepens our relationship with God. It keeps us grounded, reminding us that He is the source of all goodness, wisdom, and strength.

Ask Yourself: *Am I living with a heart of reverence for God in my daily actions and attitudes? Do I reverence Him enough in my life, at home, in relationships, in my family, in church, and every other aspect of my life? How can I reverence God more in my life right now?*

Call-to-Action: Take time today to intentionally practice reverence. Spend a moment in prayer or worship, acknowledging God's greatness and offering gratitude for His presence in your life. Let your actions reflect your deep respect for Him.

📌 **Share this word with someone who inspires you to honor God, and let's encourage one another to live with reverence and awe.**

Live with reverence today—approach God with humility and gratitude, and let His holiness shape your life.

39. TODAY'S WORD IS: DEPENDENCE

WEEK 6 DAY 4

Good morning!

Let's begin the day with a word that reminds us to lean on God: **Dependence**. Dependence is recognizing that we can't do everything on our own and trusting fully in God's strength, provision, and guidance.

A Thought to Reflect On

In **Isaiah 26:4**, we're encouraged, *"Trust in the Lord forever, for the Lord, the Lord Himself, is the Rock eternal."* This passage reminds us that God is our unshakable foundation. When we depend on Him, we find strength, stability, and peace that the world cannot provide.

Why Does It Matter to You?

Dependence matters because life often brings challenges that we cannot face alone. Trying to rely solely on our own strength can lead to frustration, fear, or burnout. However,

Dependence on God brings freedom and peace, knowing He is in control and will provide for our needs.

Dependence also strengthens our relationship with God. It's an act of faith that says, *"Lord, I trust You to handle this, even when I can't see the way forward."* Placing trust in God as your source of strength means relying on Him for all your needs, trusting that He will provide physical sustenance, emotional support, or spiritual wisdom.

Ask Yourself: *Do I depend on God in every area of my life, or are there places where I'm trying to take control?*

Call-to-Action: Identify one area of your life today where you need to depend more on God. Surrender it to Him in prayer, and trust that He will guide you and provide exactly what you need.

Share this word with someone who reminds you to rely on God, and let's encourage each other to depend more on Him.

Depend on God today—trust in His strength, lean on His promises, and let Him carry your burdens.

40. TODAY'S WORD IS: DEVOTION

WEEK 6 DAY 5

Good morning!

Let's begin the day with a word that speaks to wholehearted commitment: **Devotion**. Devotion is a deep and unwavering love for God, expressed through daily acts of worship, prayer, and obedience.

A Thought to Reflect On

Deuteronomy 6:5 instructs us, *"Love the Lord your God with all your heart and with all your soul and with all your strength."* This verse reminds us that devotion is not just a feeling—it's a way of life, putting God at the center of everything we do.

Why Does It Matter to You?

Devotion matters because it aligns your heart with God's will. It's easy to get distracted by the demands of life, but devotion calls us back to what's most important: our relationship with God. Devotion strengthens our faith, deepens our trust, and helps us stay focused on His purpose.

True devotion is expressed in our daily actions—praying, studying God's Word, serving others, and choosing to follow Him even when it's difficult.

Ask Yourself: Am I fully devoted to God, or are there aspects of my life where I feel disconnected? When was the last time I felt entirely devoted to God? What in my life right now counts as devotion to God?

Call-to-Action: Dedicate time today to deepen your devotion to God. Whether it's through prayer, reading scripture, an act of worship, or using your gifts to bless others, take a step to strengthen your relationship with Him and center your heart on His love.

Share this word with someone who inspires you to live devoted to God, and let's encourage each other to grow in faith.

Live with devotion today—love the Lord with all your heart, and let your actions reflect your commitment to Him.

41. TODAY'S WORD IS: DUTY

WEEK 6 DAY 6

Good morning!

et's begin the day with a word that calls us to fulfill our responsibilities with purpose: **Duty**. Duty is the commitment to faithfully carry out the tasks and roles God has entrusted to you, honoring Him in all you do.

A Thought to Reflect On

In **1 Corinthians 4:2**, we're reminded, *"Now it is required that those who have been given a trust must prove faithful."* This verse highlights the importance of taking our responsibilities seriously and recognizing them as opportunities to serve God and others.

Why Does It Matter to You?

Duty matters because it reflects our faithfulness to God and His trust in us. Whether in your family, work, community, or faith, fulfilling your duties with integrity and diligence brings glory to God and positively impacts those around you.

Duty is not just about doing tasks—it's about serving with a willing heart and stewardship mindset.

Ask Yourself: Do I know what my duties are? *Am I fulfilling my duties with excellence and faithfulness, or are there areas where I've been neglecting my responsibilities?*

Call-to-Action: Identify one duty or responsibility today where you can bring more focus or faithfulness. Approach it as an act of worship, committing it wholly to God and seeking to honor Him through your efforts.

Share this word with someone who inspires you to live faithfully, and let's encourage each other to fulfill our God-given duties.

Embrace your duties today—serve with purpose, diligence, and faithfulness, knowing that God is glorified in your commitment.

42. WEEKLY PAUSE: WALKING IN OBEDIENCE AND REVERENCE

WEEK 6 DAY 7

Good morning!

This week, we reflected on obedience, submission, reverence, dependence, devotion, and duty. These words remind us to align our hearts and actions with God's will, trust Him fully, and live in awe of His greatness. Let's take this moment to reflect on how these virtues have shaped our lives this week.

Reflection

- Which word resonated most deeply with you this week?
- How have these virtues encouraged you to grow in your relationship with God?
- Are there areas where you still feel God calling you to surrender or deepen your faith?

Check-In

- *What victories are you celebrating in your walk with God this week?*
- *How can you carry forward the lessons of obedience, devotion, and reverence into the coming week?*

Prayer

Lord, thank You for teaching us to walk in obedience and submission to Your will. Thank You for reminding us of the beauty of reverence, dependence, devotion, and duty. Help us to carry these lessons into the next week, honoring You in all we do and trusting Your guidance. May our lives reflect Your love, truth, and faithfulness. In Jesus' name, Amen.

**Carry these lessons into the new week
—walking in obedience, reverence,
and devotion to God's will.**

43. TODAY'S WORD IS: SACRIFICE

Good morning!

Let's begin the day with a word that calls us to greater devotion: **Sacrifice**. Sacrifice is giving up something valuable for the sake of something greater, aligning our lives with God's will and purpose.

A Thought to Reflect On

In **Romans 12:1**, we're reminded, *"Therefore, I urge you, brothers and sisters, in view of God's mercy, to offer your bodies as a living sacrifice, holy and pleasing to God—this is your true and proper worship."* This verse calls us to live a life of sacrifice, offering ourselves fully to God as an act of worship.

Why Does It Matter to You?

Sacrifice matters because it transforms us. It shifts our focus from self to God, reminding us that true fulfillment comes from living for His purpose rather than our own desires.

Sacrifice is not just about giving things up; it's about making room for God to work in and through us.

Sacrifice also reflects God's heart. Jesus' ultimate sacrifice on the cross shows us the depth of His love. When we choose sacrifice, we mirror that love in our own lives, putting God's will and the needs of others before our own.

Ask Yourself:*What is God calling me to sacrifice today? Is there an area of my life where I can surrender more fully to His will?*

Call-to-Action: Take one step of sacrifice today. It could be giving your time to help someone, setting aside a personal desire to follow God's leading, or offering a prayer of surrender. Trust that God will honor your sacrifice and use it for His glory.

Share this word with someone who inspires you to live sacrificially, and let's encourage each other to honor God with our lives.

Live sacrificially today—offer your life as a living sacrifice, holy and pleasing to God.

44. TODAY'S WORD IS: SERVICE

WEEK 7 DAY 2

Good morning!

L et's begin the day with a word that calls us to act with purpose: **Service**. Service is humbly using your time, talents, and resources to bless others and glorify God. It is a reflection of love in action.

A Thought to Reflect On

In **1 Peter 4:10**, we're reminded, *"Each of you should use whatever gift you have received to serve others as faithful stewards of God's grace in its various forms."* This verse calls us to recognize that our abilities and blessings are not just for ourselves but for serving others and advancing God's kingdom.

Why Does It Matter to You?

Service matters because it aligns us with God's heart. Jesus came not to be served but to serve, and He calls us to follow His example. Serving others is a powerful way to reflect His love, meet needs, and build relationships that point people to Him.

Service also transforms us. It shifts our focus from self to others, creating opportunities for growth, gratitude, and purpose. Whether big or small, every act of service carries eternal significance when done for God's glory.

Ask Yourself: *Am I using my gifts and blessings to glorify God and bless others? How can I serve someone today? When was the last time you served without expecting anything in return, even if it was simply wanting them to thank or praise you?*

Call-to-Action: Find one opportunity to serve today—whether by helping someone in need, offering encouragement, or volunteering your time. Approach it as an act of worship, trusting that God will use your service to make an impact.

📌 **Share this word with someone who inspires you to serve, and let's encourage each other to live with purpose and compassion.**

Serve wholeheartedly today—use your gifts to glorify God and make a difference in the lives of others.

45. TODAY'S WORD IS: STEWARDSHIP

Good morning!

Let's begin the day with a word that reminds us of our responsibility to manage well: **Stewardship**. Stewardship is the careful and faithful management of the resources, time, and gifts God has entrusted to us for His glory.

A Thought to Reflect On

In **1 Corinthians 4:2**, we're reminded, *"Now it is required that those who have been given a trust must prove faithful."* This verse highlights the importance of being trustworthy stewards of all that God has placed in our care.

Why Does It Matter to You?

Stewardship matters because everything we have—our time, talents, relationships, and possessions—comes from God. As stewards, we are called to use these blessings wisely, not for our own gain, but to honor God and serve others.

Stewardship is also an act of worship. When we faithfully manage what God has given us, we reflect our gratitude and trust in His provision.

Ask Yourself: *Am I using my resources, time, and gifts in a way that pleases God? Where can I grow in faithful stewardship?*

Call-to-Action: Take a moment today to reflect on one area of your life where you can practice better stewardship. It might be dedicating more time to God, using your gifts to serve, or being more intentional with your resources.

 Share this word with someone who inspires you to be a faithful steward, and let's encourage each other to honor God in all we manage.

Be a faithful steward today—manage God's gifts with care, gratitude, and purpose for His glory.

46. TODAY'S WORD IS: DILIGENCE

WEEK 7 DAY 4

Good morning!

Let's begin the day with a word that encourages purposeful effort: **Diligence**. Diligence is the commitment to work hard, stay focused, and persevere in fulfilling God's purpose for your life.

A Thought to Reflect On

In **Colossians 3:23**, we're reminded, *"Whatever you do, work at it with all your heart, as working for the Lord, not for human masters."* This verse calls us to approach our tasks with excellence and wholehearted dedication, viewing our work as an act of worship.

Why Does It Matter to You?

Diligence matters because it honors God and allows you to make the most of the opportunities and responsibilities He's given you. When you work diligently, you reflect God's character—He is never careless or complacent but always purposeful and faithful.

Diligence also builds resilience and helps you grow in faith. It teaches you to stay the course, even when the task feels challenging or mundane.

Ask Yourself: *Am I approaching my work and responsibilities with diligence, or are there areas where I can put more effort into it? Do I carry out my duties with due diligence?*

Call-to-Action: Identify one task or responsibility today where you can practice diligence. Whether it's in your work, relationships, or spiritual growth, commit to giving your best effort as an act of worship to God.

📌 **Share this word with someone who inspires you to live diligently, and let's encourage one another to honor God in all we do.**

Be diligent today—work with purpose, faithfulness, and a heart that glorifies God.

47. TODAY'S WORD IS: COMPASSION

WEEK 7 DAY 5

Good morning!

L et's begin the day with a word that reflects God's heart: **Compassion**. Compassion is the ability to see the needs of others and respond with love, kindness, and care, just as Jesus did.

A Thought to Reflect On

In **1 Peter 3:8**, we're reminded, *"Finally, all of you, be like-minded, be sympathetic, love one another, be compassionate and humble."* This verse calls us to actively demonstrate God's love through empathy, understanding, and acts of kindness.

Why Does It Matter to You?

Compassion matters because it mirrors God's love for us. Just as He sees our struggles and meets our needs with grace, we are called to extend that same love to others. Compassion transforms relationships and builds bridges of understanding, healing, and hope.

Compassion also deepens our faith. It moves us from simply noticing others' pain to actively being God's hands and feet in their lives.

Ask Yourself: *Am I living with a heart of compassion? How can I reflect God's love to someone in need today? When last did I show compassion to others, especially those not related to us?*

Call-to-Action: Look for an opportunity to show compassion today. Whether it's through a kind word, a thoughtful gesture, or supporting someone in a tough time, let your actions reflect God's love and care.

📌 **Share this word with someone who inspires you to live compassionately, and let's encourage each other to reflect God's heart.**

Be compassionate today—see others through God's eyes and let His love flow through your actions.

48. TODAY'S WORD IS: EMPATHY

WEEK 7 DAY 5

Good morning!

Let's begin the day with a word that calls us to connect deeply with others: **Empathy**. Empathy is the ability to understand and share the feelings of others, offering them comfort, support, and love in their struggles and joys.

A Thought to Reflect On

Romans 12:15 reminds us, *"Rejoice with those who rejoice; mourn with those who mourn."* This verse encourages us to walk alongside others, sharing in their experiences with a genuine and compassionate heart.

Why Does It Matter to You?

Empathy matters because it strengthens relationships and builds a sense of community. By stepping into someone else's shoes, you reflect God's love and show them that they are seen, valued, and not alone.

Empathy also helps us grow spiritually by teaching us humility and compassion. It reminds us that we're all part of God's family, called to support one another in love and understanding.

Ask Yourself: *Am I taking the time to truly understand the people around me? How can I show empathy today?*

Call-to-Action: Practice empathy today by actively listening to someone's story, offering encouragement, or simply being present in their moment of need. Let your actions reflect God's love and understanding.

Share this word with someone who inspires you to live with empathy, and let's encourage one another to connect more deeply with those around us.

Live with empathy today—listen, understand, and walk alongside others with God's love in your heart.

49. WEEKLY PAUSE: SERVING WITH DUE DILIGENCE

WEEK 7 DAY 7

Good morning!

This week, we reflected on sacrifice, service, stewardship, diligence, compassion, and empathy. These words remind us of the call to serve with purpose, managing our God-given responsibilities with care and love while connecting deeply with those around us. Let's take this moment to reflect on how these lessons have shaped our hearts and actions.

Reflection

- Which word inspired you the most this week to serve God and others?
- How has practicing diligence and stewardship brought greater meaning to your daily life?
- Are there areas where God calls you to deepen your

commitment to serving others with care and empathy?

Check-In

- *What victories or progress are you celebrating this week?*
- *What steps can you take to live with greater diligence and faithfulness in the week ahead?*

Prayer

Lord, thank You for teaching us the importance of serving with diligence and stewardship. Thank You for showing us how to reflect Your love through compassion and empathy. Help us carry these lessons into the coming week, managing all that You've entrusted to us with faithfulness and care. May our service bring glory to Your name and draw others closer to You. In Jesus' name, Amen.

Move forward this week, diligently serving and honoring God in every task and interaction.

50. TODAY'S WORD IS: KNOWLEDGE

Good morning!

Let's begin the day with a word that guides our communication and actions: **Knowledge**. Knowledge is more than information—it's the understanding and application of God's truth in our daily lives, especially in how we communicate with others.

A Thought to Reflect On

In **Proverbs 15:7**, we're reminded, *"The lips of the wise spread knowledge, but the hearts of fools are not upright."* This verse highlights the importance of using knowledge to speak wisely, with words that reflect God's wisdom and bring value to those around us.

Why Does It Matter to You?

Knowledge matters because it shapes how we interact with the world and the people in our lives. When we root our communication in God's Word, we become a source of wisdom, encouragement, and truth for others.

Knowledge also deepens our relationship with God, allowing us to understand His will and apply it to our actions. It helps us discern when to speak, what to say, and how to listen with grace and understanding.

Ask Yourself: *Am I using knowledge to glorify God in my words and actions? How can I grow in wisdom today?*

Call-to-Action: Spend time in God's Word today, seeking knowledge that can guide your communication and choices. Ask God for wisdom to speak words that honor Him and build others up.

Share this word with someone who inspires you to seek and share God's wisdom, and let's encourage each other to grow in knowledge.

Speak with knowledge today—let your words reflect God's truth and bring light to those around you.

51. TODAY'S WORD IS: LISTENING

WEEK 8 DAY 2

Good morning!

Let's begin the day with a word that fosters connection and understanding: **Listening**. Listening is not just hearing—it's giving your full attention to God and others, showing that you value their words and their hearts.

A Thought to Reflect On

In **James 1:19**, we're reminded, *"My dear brothers and sisters, take note of this: Everyone should be quick to listen, slow to speak, and slow to become angry."* This verse calls us to prioritize listening over speaking, creating space for understanding and wisdom.

Why Does It Matter to You?

Listening matters because it strengthens relationships. When we listen well, we show respect and care, deepening our connection with others. Listening also allows us to hear

God's voice in prayer, scripture, and the stillness of our hearts.

True listening requires humility and patience. It's about setting aside distractions, suspending judgment, and focusing entirely on the speaker.

Ask Yourself: *Am I truly listening to God and others, or am I too quick to respond or interrupt?*

Call-to-Action: Practice intentional listening today. Take time to hear someone out without interrupting, and spend quiet moments in prayer, asking God to speak to your heart.

📌 **Share this word with someone who inspires you to be a better listener, and let's encourage each other to connect more deeply through listening.**

Listen with intention today—open your heart to God's guidance and the voices of those around you.

52. TODAY'S WORD IS: UNDERSTANDING

WEEK 8 DAY 3

Good morning!

Let's begin the day with a word that builds bridges and fosters peace: **Understanding**. Understanding goes beyond hearing—it's about seeing through the eyes of others, connecting with their experiences, and seeking clarity in all interactions.

A Thought to Reflect On

In **Proverbs 20:5,** we're reminded, *"The purposes of a person's heart are deep waters, but one who has insight draws them out."* This verse calls us to approach others with patience and discernment, drawing out their thoughts and emotions with wisdom and care.

Why Does It Matter to You?

Understanding matters because it creates connection and fosters trust. It allows us to bridge differences, resolve conflicts, and show empathy in our relationships. We reflect God's love and humility in our interactions by seeking understanding.

Understanding also enriches our relationship with God. When we seek His wisdom, we gain insight into His plans for our lives and how to better love and serve others.

Ask Yourself: *Am I approaching conversations with a desire to understand, or am I focused on getting my own point across?*

Call-to-Action: Today, approach your interactions with a heart of understanding. Take time to ask thoughtful questions, listen deeply, and seek clarity before responding. Let your words and actions reflect God's love and wisdom.

📌 **Share this word with someone who inspires you to live with understanding, and let's encourage each other to build deeper connections.**

Seek understanding today—be patient, listen with care, and let God's wisdom guide your heart.

53. TODAY'S WORD IS: WORDS

Good morning!

Let's begin the day with a word that holds immense power: **Words**. Words can build up or tear down, heal or hurt, encourage or discourage. They are a reflection of what is in our hearts and a tool God has given us to share His love and truth.

A Thought to Reflect On

In **Proverbs 18:21**, we're reminded, *"The tongue has the power of life and death, and those who love it will eat its fruit."* This verse emphasizes the impact of our words, calling us to use them wisely and with care.

Why Does It Matter to You?

Words matter because they shape relationships and influence the world around us. Kind and thoughtful words can inspire hope, strengthen bonds, and reflect God's love. Careless or harsh words, however, can damage trust and wound others.

As followers of Christ, we're called to speak words that build up and encourage, reflecting His truth and grace.

Ask Yourself: *Am I using my words to bring life and light to others, or am I being careless with what I say?*

Call-to-Action: Today, choose your words intentionally. Speak life into someone's day with encouragement or kindness. Before speaking, pause and ask yourself: *Will my words reflect God's love?*

 Share this word with someone who inspires you to speak wisely, and let's encourage each other to use words to glorify God.

Let your words bring life today—speak with kindness, truth, and love, reflecting God's heart in every conversation.

54. TODAY'S WORD IS: ENCOURAGEMENT

Good morning!

Let's begin the day with a word that uplifts and inspires: **Encouragement**. Encouragement is the act of using words and actions to build others up, offering hope and strength in times of need.

A Thought to Reflect On

In **1 Thessalonians 5:11**, we're reminded, *"Therefore encourage one another and build each other up, just as in fact you are doing."* This verse calls us to be intentional in lifting others, sharing God's love through words that inspire and strengthen.

Why Does It Matter to You?

Encouragement matters because it has the power to transform lives. A kind word, a thoughtful gesture, or simply showing someone that you care can brighten their day and renew their hope. Encouragement fosters connection and reminds others they are not alone in their struggles.

As followers of Christ, we are called to be a source of encouragement, reflecting God's faithfulness and grace.

Ask Yourself: *How can I use my words and actions to encourage someone today?*

Call-to-Action: Take a moment today to encourage someone. It could be through a compliment, a prayer, or simply being present for them. Let your encouragement reflect God's love and inspire them to keep moving forward.

📌 **Share this word with someone who inspires you to encourage others, and let's lift each other up in faith and love.**

Encourage someone today—use your words and actions to bring hope and reflect God's love.

55. TODAY'S WORD IS: CLARITY

WEEK 8 DAY 6

Good morning!

Let's begin the day with a word that emphasizes truth and understanding: **Clarity**. Clarity is speaking and living in a way that reflects God's truth, ensuring that our words and actions align with His will and purpose.

A Thought to Reflect On

In **Matthew 5:37**, Jesus teaches, *"Let your 'Yes' be 'Yes,' and your 'No,' 'No'; anything beyond this comes from the evil one."* This verse reminds us of the importance of honesty and simplicity in our communication, ensuring that our words are clear and trustworthy.

Why Does It Matter to You?

Clarity matters because it builds trust and fosters understanding in our relationships. When we communicate clearly, we reflect God's truth and avoid misunderstandings or confusion. Clarity also strengthens our witness, showing others that our words and actions are consistent with our faith.

Clarity begins in the heart—when we are aligned with God's truth, our communication reflects His love and wisdom.

Ask Yourself: *Am I speaking and living with clarity, or are there areas where I need to be more honest and transparent?*

Call-to-Action: Today, practice clarity in your conversations. Speak truthfully and simply, ensuring that your words reflect God's love and wisdom. Let your communication build trust and understanding with those around you.

Share this word with someone who inspires you to live with clarity, and let's encourage each other to speak and act in truth.

Communicate with clarity today—let your words and actions reflect the simplicity and truth of God's love.

56. WEEKLY PAUSE: COMMUNICATING WITH UNDERSTANDING AND GRACE

WEEK 8 DAY 7

Good morning!

This week, we explored knowledge, listening, understanding, words, encouragement, and clarity. These themes remind us of the power of communication in building relationships and reflecting God's love. Let's take this moment to reflect on how these lessons have shaped our hearts and actions this week.

Reflection

- Which word spoke most deeply to you this week?
- How did practicing these virtues improve your connection with God and others?
- Are there areas where you feel God is calling you to grow in your communication?
- Where do you start from?

Check-In

- *What victories are you celebrating in communicating with understanding and grace this week?*
- *How can you carry forward the lessons of clear, loving communication into the next week?*

Prayer

Lord, thank You for teaching us the value of communication that reflects Your truth and love. Thank You for showing us how to listen, speak clearly, and encourage others gracefully. Help us to carry these lessons forward, using our words to build trust, foster connection, and honor You in all we do. In Jesus' name, Amen.

Step into the new week with a heart for understanding, words of encouragement, and a commitment to communicate with grace and clarity.

57. TODAY'S WORD IS: LEADERSHIP

WEEK 9 DAY 1

Good morning!

Let's begin the day with a word that inspires action and service: **Leadership**. Leadership isn't about position or power—it's about serving others, guiding with wisdom, and reflecting God's heart in every decision.

A Thought to Reflect On

In **Matthew 20:26**, Jesus teaches, *"Whoever wants to become great among you must be your servant."* This verse reminds us that true leadership is rooted in humility and service, putting the needs of others above our own and leading by example.

Why Does It Matter to You?

Leadership matters because it impacts those around you. Whether you're leading a team, your family, or simply influencing others through your actions, leadership reflects your values and priorities. God calls us to lead with integrity, humility, and a heart of service, just as Jesus did.

Leadership also deepens your relationship with God as you seek His guidance and strength.

Ask Yourself: *Am I leading in a way that honors God? How can I better serve and uplift those around me?*

Call-to-Action: Take one step today to lead with humility and purpose. Let your actions reflect God's heart, whether it's offering support, making a thoughtful decision, or guiding someone with care.

Share this word with someone who inspires you to lead with integrity, and let's encourage each other to be servant leaders.

Lead with purpose today—serve others, guide with humility, and honor God in all you do.

58. TODAY'S WORD IS: INFLUENCE

WEEK 9 DAY 2

Good morning!

Let's begin the day with a word that highlights the power of your actions: **Influence**. Influence is the ability to inspire and impact others through your words, choices, and examples, reflecting God's light in every interaction.

A Thought to Reflect On

In **Matthew 5:16**, Jesus says, *"Let your light shine before others, that they may see your good deeds and glorify your Father in heaven."* This verse reminds us that our influence is not for personal gain but to point others toward God's love and truth.

Why Does It Matter to You?

Influence matters because it shapes the world around you. Whether through big actions or small gestures, your influence can inspire change, foster hope, and bring others closer to God.

As believers, we are called to use our influence intentionally, not carelessly. Living with integrity and love reflects God's character and encourages others to do the same.

Ask Yourself: *Am I using my influence to glorify God and uplift those around me?*

Call-to-Action: Be intentional about your influence today. Choose one action—whether it's encouraging someone, making a selfless decision, or leading by example—that reflects God's love and inspires those around you.

 Share this word with someone who influences you in a positive way, and let's encourage each other to be lights in the world.

Let your influence shine today—use your words and actions to glorify God and inspire others.

59. TODAY'S WORD IS: COMMITMENT

WEEK 9 DAY 3

Good morning!

Let's begin the day with a word that reflects steadfast dedication: **Commitment**. Commitment is remaining faithful to your responsibilities, relationships, and faith, even when challenges arise or the path becomes difficult.

A Thought to Reflect On

In **Proverbs 16:3**, we're reminded, *"Commit your work to the Lord, and your plans will be established."* This verse calls us to put our trust and efforts in God's hands, knowing He will guide and bless our dedication.

Why Does It Matter to You?

Commitment matters because it builds trust and strengthens your character. It reflects God's unwavering love and faithfulness, reminding others of His reliability.

Whether it's in your work, relationships, or spiritual growth, commitment is a testimony to God's presence in your life.

Commitment also deepens your connection to God. By staying faithful to Him, even in the small things, you create space for His will to unfold in your life.

Ask Yourself: *Am I fully committed to the tasks and relationships God has placed in my life? How can I demonstrate greater faithfulness today?*

Call-to-Action: Identify one area in your life where you can strengthen your commitment today. Whether it's dedicating time to prayer, being intentional in a relationship, or fulfilling a responsibility with excellence, let your actions reflect your faithfulness to God.

Share this word with someone who inspires you to stay committed, and let's encourage each other to live with dedication and faith.

Stay committed today—trust in God's plans and reflect His faithfulness in all you do.

60. TODAY'S WORD IS: ADAPTABILITY

Good morning!

Let's begin the day with a word that calls us to trust and flexibility: **Adaptability**. Adaptability is adjusting to changes and challenges and trusting God's plan even when life doesn't go as expected.

A Thought to Reflect On:

In **Philippians 4:12**, Paul writes, *"I know what it is to be in need, and I know what it is to have plenty. I have learned the secret of being content in any and every situation."* This verse reminds us that adaptability is rooted in faith—finding contentment and peace by trusting God in all circumstances.

Why Does It Matter to You?

Adaptability matters because life is unpredictable. Challenges and changes can be unsettling, but adaptability allows you to remain steady and hopeful, trusting that God is in control.

Adaptability also helps you grow in faith and resilience. When you embrace change with an open heart, you allow God to shape you and use every situation for His purpose.

Ask Yourself: *Am I resisting change, or am I trusting God's plan and adapting with faith?*

Call-to-Action: Today, embrace a change or challenge with adaptability. Instead of resisting, pray for God's guidance and trust Him to lead you through it. Let your flexibility reflect your faith in His plan.

📌 **Share this word with someone who inspires you to adapt gracefully and encourage each other to trust God in all seasons.**

Be adaptable today—trust God's plan, embrace change, and grow in faith and resilience.

61. TODAY'S WORD IS: TEAMWORK

WEEK 9 DAY 5

Good morning!

Let's begin the day with a word emphasizing unity and collaboration: **Teamwork**. Teamwork is about working together with others toward a shared goal, supporting and strengthening each other along the way.

A Thought to Reflect On

In **Ecclesiastes 4:9**, we're reminded, *"Two are better than one because they have a good return for their labor."* This verse highlights the power of collaboration and the value of working together in unity, combining strengths to achieve greater results.

Why Does It Matter to You?

Teamwork matters because we are not meant to go through life alone. God designed us to live and work in a community, helping and encouraging one another. When we practice teamwork, we reflect His love by putting others first and valuing their contributions.

Teamwork also strengthens our faith. It teaches us humility, patience, and the beauty of shared victories.

Ask Yourself: *Am I contributing to the teams in my life with a spirit of collaboration and support? How can I strengthen my role in those partnerships today?*

Call-to-Action: Find one opportunity today to contribute to teamwork—whether it's in your family, workplace, or church. Offer support, encouragement, or collaboration, and let your actions reflect God's heart for unity.

 Share this word with someone who inspires you to value teamwork, and let's encourage one another to work together in faith and purpose.

Practice teamwork today—build connections, share strengths, and reflect God's love through unity.

62. TODAY'S WORD IS: UNITY

WEEK 9 DAY 6

Good morning!

Let's begin the day with a word that brings us together: **Unity**. Unity is the bond that connects us in love, trust, and shared purpose, reflecting God's desire for His people to live in harmony.

A Thought to Reflect On

In **Ephesians 4:3**, we're reminded, *"Make every effort to keep the unity of the Spirit through the bond of peace."* This verse calls us to actively pursue unity, valuing peace and understanding as we work together for God's purpose.

Why Does It Matter to You?

Unity matters because it strengthens relationships and builds community. When we live in unity, we reflect God's love and demonstrate the power of His Spirit working among us. Unity fosters peace, trust, and a shared sense of purpose.

Unity also reminds us that we are stronger together. By setting aside differences and focusing on what unites us—our faith and love for God—we become a powerful witness to the world.

Ask Yourself: *Am I promoting unity in my relationships, or are there areas where I need to foster greater peace and connection?*

Call-to-Action: Today, take one step to promote unity. Whether it's resolving a conflict, offering forgiveness, or simply encouraging someone, let your actions reflect God's desire for harmony and love among His people.

Share this word with someone who inspires you to live in unity, and let's encourage each other to build stronger connections in faith.

Live in unity today—pursue peace, foster connection,
and reflect God's love in all you do.

63. WEEKLY PAUSE: LEADING WITH UNITY AND PURPOSE

WEEK 9 DAY 7

Good morning!

This week, we reflected on leadership, influence, commitment, adaptability, teamwork, and unity. These words remind us of the importance of serving others, working together, and staying faithful to God's purpose in every aspect of our lives. Let's take this moment to pause and reflect on how these lessons have shaped our week.

Reflection

- Which word resonated most deeply with you this week?
- How did practicing these virtues impact your relationships and your connection with God?
- Are there areas in your life where God is calling you to grow as a leader or team member?

Check-In

- *What victories are you celebrating this week?*
- *How can you continue to foster unity and purpose in your relationships and actions next week?*

Prayer

Lord, thank You for teaching us the value of leadership rooted in humility, influence guided by love, and commitment to Your purpose. Thank You for showing us the beauty of adaptability, teamwork, and unity in building stronger relationships and communities. Help us carry these lessons into the week ahead, leading with purpose and reflecting Your heart in all we do. In Jesus' name, Amen.

Move forward into the next week with a heart of unity, a spirit of service, and a commitment to living out God's purpose.

64. TODAY'S WORD IS: CHANGE

Good morning!

Let's begin the day with a word that stirs our hearts and challenges our comfort: **Change**. Change is the bridge between where we are and where God wants to take us. It's often unsettling, sometimes unexpected, but always an invitation to grow and trust in the One who holds the future.

A Thought to Reflect On

In **Ecclesiastes 3:1**, we're reminded, *"There is a time for everything and a season for every activity under the heavens."* This verse reassures us that change is not random but a part of God's divine design. Every season has a purpose, even when we can't see it immediately.

Why Does It Matter to You?

Change matters because it shifts our perspective and strengthens our faith. It teaches us to release control and lean into God's plan, trusting that He is working all things for our good.

Instead of fearing change, we can embrace it as God's way of stretching us and leading us into something greater.

Ask Yourself: *Am I welcoming change as part of God's plan, or am I resisting the growth He's calling me to?*

Call-to-Action: Choose to embrace change today. Reflect on one area of your life where God might be calling you to trust Him more. Take a small step of faith, knowing He is with you in every transition.

📌 **Share this word with someone facing change, and let's encourage one another to walk boldly in faith.**

Step into change today—trust God's timing, embrace the journey, and let Him guide you into His perfect plan.

65. TODAY'S WORD IS: ACCEPTANCE

WEEK 10 DAY 2

Good morning!

Let's begin the day with a word that calms our hearts: **Acceptance**. Acceptance is not about giving up; it's about releasing the need to control what we cannot change and trusting God to work all things for good. It's the quiet strength of faith that says, *"Lord, I trust You, even in this."*

A Thought to Reflect On

In **Psalm 46:10**, we're reminded, *"He says, 'Be still, and know that I am God.'"* This verse calls us to find peace in God's sovereignty. When we stop striving to control every outcome, we make space for His power and grace to guide us.

Why Does It Matter to You?

Acceptance matters because it frees you from the burden of trying to change what is beyond your control. It allows you to focus on what you can do while trusting God with what you cannot.

Acceptance isn't passive; it's an active choice to surrender your fears, anxieties, and uncertainties to God, knowing that His plans are greater than yours.

Ask Yourself: *What am I holding onto too tightly? Where do I need to practice acceptance and trust today?*

Call-to-Action: Identify one area in your life where you need to practice acceptance. Take it to God in prayer and release it into His hands, trusting His wisdom and love to lead you forward.

📌 **Share this word with someone who needs peace, and let's encourage each other to accept God's plans with faith and grace.**

Embrace acceptance today—release what you cannot control and trust the One who holds it all.

66. TODAY'S WORD IS: PERSPECTIVE

WEEK 10 DAY 3

Good morning!

Let's begin the day with a word that shifts our focus: **Perspective**. Perspective is the lens through which we view life's challenges and blessings. When we adopt God's perspective, we see beyond the momentary struggles and glimpse His eternal purpose.

A Thought to Reflect On

In **Colossians 3:2**, we're reminded, *"Set your minds on things above, not on earthly things."* This verse encourages us to lift our eyes from the temporary and focus on the eternal. Even in uncertain times, God's perspective brings clarity, peace, and hope.

Why Does It Matter to You?

Perspective matters because it changes how you respond to life. When you see challenges through God's eyes, they become growth opportunities. When you view blessings with gratitude, they deepen your joy. Perspective helps you align your thoughts with God's truth, anchoring your heart in His promises.

Ask Yourself: *Am I viewing my circumstances through God's perspective, or am I stuck in a narrow, earthly view? How can I shift my focus today?*

Call-to-Action:

Take a moment today to ask God for His perspective on a challenge or situation in your life. Reflect on how His Word and promises reshape the way you see your circumstances.

📌 **Share this word with someone who inspires you to look at life through a faith-filled lens, and let's encourage each other to seek God's perspective.**

Shift your perspective today—see life through God's eyes, and let His truth guide your heart.

67. TODAY'S WORD IS: FLEXIBILITY

WEEK 10 DAY 4

Good morning!

Let's begin the day with a word that encourages openness: **Flexibility**. Flexibility is the willingness to adapt when plans change, trusting that God's purpose will always prevail. It's the posture of faith that says, *"Lord, lead me where You will."*

A Thought to Reflect On

In **Proverbs 19:21**, we're reminded, *"Many are the plans in a person's heart, but it is the Lord's purpose that prevails."* This verse teaches us that while we may have our own plans, true peace comes from surrendering to God's greater plan, even when it requires us to adjust.

Why Does It Matter to You?

Flexibility matters because life is unpredictable. Unexpected changes can cause frustration, but a flexible spirit allows you to embrace those changes with trust and grace. It also opens your heart to new opportunities that God may place before you.

Flexibility strengthens your faith by teaching you to rely on God rather than your own understanding.

Ask Yourself: *Am I clinging too tightly to my plans, or am I open to the direction God is leading me?*

Call-to-Action: Practice flexibility today by responding to any changes or interruptions with patience and trust. Take a moment to pray for God's guidance in navigating the unexpected with faith.

Share this word with someone who inspires you to stay open to God's plans, and let's encourage one another to trust His purpose.

Be flexible today—embrace life's changes as opportunities to grow closer to God and align with His will.

68. TODAY'S WORD IS: TRANSFORMATION

WEEK 10 DAY 5

Good morning!

Let's begin the day with a word that signifies growth and renewal: **Transformation**. Transformation is a profound process in which we are molded and transformed by God's divine intervention, guiding us to reflect His image and fulfill His purpose. It is an ongoing journey that involves shedding the remnants of our former selves and wholeheartedly embracing the new dimensions of our spiritual existence.

A Thought to Reflect On

In **Romans 12:2**, we're reminded, *"Do not conform to the pattern of this world but be transformed by the renewing of your mind. Then you will be able to test and approve what God's will is —His good, pleasing, and perfect will."* This verse warmly encourages us to embrace profound transformation as God refreshes and revitalizes our minds and attitudes, guiding us toward a more enlightened and positive perspective.

Why Does It Matter to You?

Transformation matters because it reflects God's ongoing work in your life. It's a process of becoming more like Christ, allowing His love, wisdom, and grace to shine through you. Transformation often comes through challenges, but each step brings you closer to His purpose.

Ask Yourself: *Where is God calling me to grow and change? Am I allowing Him to transform my heart, or am I resisting His work?*

Call-to-Action: Spend time today reflecting on an area of your life where God may be calling you to transform. Surrender it to Him in prayer, asking for His guidance and strength to grow into the person He's shaping you to be.

📌 **Share this word with someone who inspires you to embrace change, and let's encourage one another to allow God to transform us.**

Embrace transformation today—let God renew your mind, shape your heart, and guide you into His perfect will.

69. TODAY'S WORD IS: GROWTH

WEEK 10 DAY 6

Good morning!

Let's begin the day with a word that reflects progress and purpose: **Growth**. Growth is the evidence of life—it's the process of becoming more of who God created you to be spiritually, emotionally, and personally.

A Thought to Reflect On

In **Philippians 1:6**, we're reminded, *"Being confident of this, that He who began a good work in you will carry it on to completion until the day of Christ Jesus."* This verse reassures us that God is constantly working in us, helping us grow into His purpose and plan.

Why Does It Matter to You?

Growth matters because it shows that we are moving forward, even in the face of challenges. Each day is an opportunity to learn, to deepen our faith, and to draw closer to

God. Growth doesn't happen overnight—it's a gradual process that requires trust, patience, and persistence.

Ask Yourself: *Am I embracing opportunities to grow, or am I staying in my comfort zone? How can I take one step toward growth today?*

Call-to-Action:

Identify one area in your life where you'd like to grow—whether it's spiritually, emotionally, or in your relationships. Take a small but intentional step toward progress today, trusting God to guide you.

📌 **Share this word with someone who inspires you to keep growing, and let's encourage each other to step into God's purpose.**

**Step into growth today
—trust God to nurture and shape you, becoming more of
who He created you to be.**

70. Weekly Pause: Navigating Change with Transformation and Growth

Good morning!

This week, we reflected on change, acceptance, perspective, flexibility, transformation, and growth. These words remind us of the beauty and purpose of embracing change, trusting God's plans, and allowing Him to work in and through us. Let's take this moment to pause and reflect on the lessons we've learned this week.

Reflection

- Which word resonated most deeply with you this week?
- How have you seen God at work in the changes or challenges you've faced recently?
- Are there areas in your life where God is calling you to be more open to transformation or growth?

Check-In

- *What progress are you celebrating this week?*
- *What steps can you take to embrace change more fully in the future?*

Prayer

Lord, thank You for teaching us to embrace change with trust and hope. Thank You for showing us the beauty of acceptance, the strength of perspective, and the power of transformation and growth. Help us carry these lessons into the next week, trusting in Your plans and allowing You to guide us through every season. May our lives continue to reflect Your love and purpose. In Jesus' name, Amen.

Step into the new week with faith, trusting God to lead you through every change and transform your heart for His glory.

71. TODAY'S WORD IS: TOUGHER

WEEK 11 DAY 1

Good morning!

Let's begin the day with a word that challenges us to endure and grow: **Tougher.** Being tougher doesn't simply equate to being hard-hearted or devoid of emotions; instead, it is about cultivating a deep resilience through faith. It involves learning how to steadfastly endure the tempests of life while maintaining a gentle, compassionate heart attuned to God's leading and love. This balance allows you to face challenges with strength yet remain open and sensitive to the divine presence in your life.

A Thought to Reflect On

In **John 16:33**, Jesus reminds us, *"I have told you these things, so that in Me you may have peace. In this world, you will have trouble. But take heart! I have overcome the world."* This verse reminds us that while life's challenges are inevitable, our ability to endure comes from knowing that Jesus has already won the ultimate victory.

Why Does It Matter to You?

Being tougher matters because life will test your faith, patience, and perseverance. Toughness, rooted in God's strength, allows you to face difficulties without breaking. It's not about avoiding hardship but about trusting God to see you through it.

Ask Yourself: *Am I relying on my own strength to endure, or am I trusting God to make me tougher in faith and spirit?*

Call-to-Action: Today, face one challenge with a mindset of faith and endurance. Instead of shrinking back, lean into God's promises, knowing that He is shaping you into someone stronger and more reliant on His grace.

📌 **Share this word with someone who inspires you to stay tough in faith, and let's encourage one another to persevere through God's strength.**

Be tougher today—stand firm in God's promises, face challenges boldly, and trust Him to see you through.

72. TODAY'S WORD IS: STRONGER

WEEK 11 DAY 2

Good morning!

Let's begin the day with a word that reflects growth through challenges: **Stronger**. Strength isn't just about physical endurance—it's about becoming spiritually, emotionally, and mentally fortified through God's grace and guidance.

A Thought to Reflect On

In **James 1:2-3**, we're reminded, *"Consider it pure joy, my brothers and sisters, whenever you face trials of many kinds, because you know that the testing of your faith produces perseverance."* This verse powerfully illustrates that true strength is forged in the crucible of adversity, where each challenging trial serves as a stepping stone, bringing us ever closer to becoming the individuals that God is meticulously shaping us to be.

Why Does It Matter to You?

Becoming stronger matters because life's challenges are inevitable. Strength isn't about avoiding hardship but about allowing God to use it to refine and prepare you for more incredible things. Strength through faith helps you remain steadfast and courageous, even when the path is unclear.

Ask Yourself: *Am I allowing life's challenges to strengthen me in faith and character, or am I resisting the growth God wants for me?*

Call-to-Action: Identify one area of your life where you can choose strength today. Whether it's through perseverance, forgiveness, or trusting God with a difficult situation, take a step toward becoming stronger through His power.

🕊 **Share this word with someone who inspires you to grow stronger in faith, and let's encourage each other to embrace growth through challenges.**

Be stronger today—let God's grace and strength sustain you, and trust that He is working through every trial.

73. TODAY'S WORD IS: BETTER

WEEK 11 DAY 3

Good morning!

Let's begin the day with a word that inspires improvement: **Better**. Better isn't about perfection—it's about progress, choosing growth over stagnation, and allowing God to shape you into who He created you to be.

A Thought to Reflect On

In **Romans 8:28**, we're reminded, *"And we know that in all things God works for the good of those who love Him, who have been called according to His purpose."* This verse assures us that even in difficult times, God is working to make things better, using every experience to refine and strengthen us.

Why Does It Matter to You?

Choosing to be better matters because it reflects your willingness to grow, learn, and trust God's plan. Life will present opportunities to either grow bitter from hardship or better through faith. When you strive to be better, you open yourself to God's transformative work in your life.

Ask Yourself: *Am I allowing God to use my experiences to make me better? How can I choose growth and grace today?*

Call-to-Action: Focus on one small way you can be better today—whether it's through kindness, patience, forgiveness, or gratitude. Let God guide you in making progress toward who He's calling you to be.

📌 **Share this word with someone who inspires you to grow and be better, and let's encourage each other to walk in faith and grace.**

Be better today—trust God to use every moment to refine and strengthen you, becoming more of who He created you to be.

74. TODAY'S WORD IS: EMPOWERED

WEEK 11 DAY 4

Morning!

Let's begin the day with a word that ignites confidence: **Empowered**. To be empowered is to live boldly, knowing that God equips you with the strength, wisdom, and courage to face every challenge and fulfill His purpose for your life.

A Thought to Reflect On

In **2 Timothy 1:7**, we're reminded, *"For the Spirit God gave us does not make us timid, but gives us power, love, and self-discipline."* This verse declares that God's Spirit empowers us to live with boldness, guided by love and rooted in discipline, enabling us to walk in His purpose without fear.

Why Does It Matter to You?

Feeling empowered matters because it shifts your mindset from doubt to faith. It reminds you that you're not walking through life's challenges alone—God's Spirit is within you, giving you the tools you need to overcome obstacles and make a difference.

Ask Yourself: *Am I living as someone empowered by God's Spirit, or am I letting fear and doubt hold me back?*

Call-to-Action: Step into empowerment today by trusting God with a decision or challenge that feels overwhelming. Remind yourself that He has equipped you with everything you need to succeed and glorify Him in the process.

Share this word with someone who inspires you to live boldly, and let's encourage each other to walk confidently in God's power.

Live empowered today—embrace the Spirit God has given you, and let His strength and love guide your actions.

75. TODAY'S WORD IS: OVERCOMER

WEEK 11 DAY 5

Good morning!

Let's begin the day with a word that speaks to triumph: **Overcomer**. An overcomer is someone who faces challenges head-on, rooted in faith and trusting God to bring victory in every situation.

A Thought to Reflect On

In **Romans 8:37**, we're reminded, *"No, in all these things, we are more than conquerors through Him who loved us."* This verse declares that through Christ, we are not just survivors—we are overcomers equipped to rise above trials with His love and strength.

Why Does It Matter to You?

Being an overcomer matters because life will present battles, but victory is promised through Christ. As an overcomer, you live not in fear or defeat but in the assurance that God's power is greater than any obstacle you face.

Ask Yourself: *Am I living as an overcomer, trusting God to lead me to victory, or am I letting fear and doubt hold me back?*

Call-to-Action: Embrace your identity as an overcomer today. Face one challenge with the confidence that God is fighting for you and will lead you to victory. Declare His promises over your situation and trust in His power.

📌 **Share this word with someone who inspires you to live victoriously, and let's encourage one another to embrace our identity as overcomers.**

Live as an overcomer today—trust God to lead you through every challenge and into His perfect victory.

76. TODAY'S WORD IS: VICTORIOUS

WEEK 11 DAY 6

Good morning!

Let's begin the day with a word that inspires triumph: **Victorious**. Victory is not just about winning battles—it's about walking in the assurance that, through Christ, you have already overcome the ultimate challenges of life.

A Thought to Reflect On

In **1 Corinthians 15:57**, we're reminded, *"But thanks be to God! He gives us the victory through our Lord Jesus Christ."* This verse reminds us that victory is a gift from God, not something we earn. Through Jesus, we are victorious over sin, fear, and even death.

Why Does It Matter to You?

Living victoriously matters because it shifts your mindset. Instead of striving for victory, you live from a place of victory—knowing that God has already secured it for you. This confidence allows you to face life's challenges with hope, courage, and trust in His promises.

Ask Yourself: *Am I walking in the victory Christ has given me, or am I living in fear and defeat? How can I claim His promises more boldly today?*

Call-to-Action: Step into victory today by declaring God's promises over your life. Let go of fear or doubt, and face your day with the confidence that Christ has already won the battle.

📌 **Share this word with someone who inspires you to live victoriously, and let's encourage one another to walk in God's promises.**

Live victoriously today—walk boldly in the freedom, joy, and strength that Christ has secured for you.

77. WEEKLY PAUSE: BECOMING TOUGHER, BETTER, AND VICTORIOUS THROUGH FAITH

WEEK 11 DAY 7

Good morning!

This week, we reflected on toughness, strength, empowerment, and victory. These words remind us of God's power at work within us, shaping us to face life's challenges with faith and courage. Let's take this moment to pause and reflect on the ways God is refining and strengthening us.

Reflection

- Which word from this week spoke most deeply to your heart?
- How have you seen God at work in your ability to overcome challenges and grow stronger in faith?
- Are there areas where you feel God calling you to trust Him more boldly as you walk in victory?

Check-In

- *What progress are you celebrating in becoming tougher, stronger, and more faith-driven this week?*
- *What steps can you take to fully embrace your identity as an overcomer in Christ?*

Prayer

Lord, thank You for teaching us how to become tougher, stronger, and better through Your love and grace. Thank You for empowering us to overcome life's challenges and walk in the victory You've already secured for us. Help us carry these lessons into the next week, living boldly, trusting Your promises, and reflecting Your strength in all we do. In Jesus' name, Amen.

Step into the next week confidently, trusting God to make you tougher, better, and victorious for His glory.

78. TODAY'S WORD IS: ABLE

WEEK 12 DAY 1

Good morning!

Let's begin the day with a word that empowers us: **Able**. To be able is to recognize that God equips and strengthens you to face challenges, fulfill your purpose, and live abundantly in His grace.

A Thought to Reflect On

2 Corinthians 9:8 reminds us, *"And God is capable of blessing you abundantly, so that in every situation and at all times, having everything you need, you will thrive in every good work."* This verse reassures us that God meets our needs and empowers us to succeed in all He asks of us do.

Why Does It Matter to You?

Knowing that you are able is realizing that your inherent strengths and unique abilities are not the barriers that constrain you. Instead, they remind you of the vast potential that resides within you, encouraging you to reach beyond your perceived limitations and strive for greater achievements. God's power works through you, making you capable of achieving more than you could on your own. When you rely on Him, you can overcome obstacles, face fears, and accomplish great things for His glory.

Ask Yourself: *Do I trust in God's ability to work through me, or am I holding back because of fear or doubt? How can I lean into His strength today?*

Call-to-Action: Step into your day confidently, knowing God has made you able. Take on a challenge or task with faith that His strength will guide and sustain you.

🦋 **Share this word with someone who inspires you to believe in God's ability to empower them, and let's encourage one another to live boldly.**

Walk confidently today—God has made you able to face any challenge and accomplish His purpose.

79. TODAY'S WORD IS: POSITIVE

WEEK 12 DAY 2

Good morning!

Let's begin the day with a word that uplifts our mindset: **Positive**. A positive attitude doesn't ignore challenges—it focuses on God's goodness, His promises, and the blessings He places in every situation.

A Thought to Reflect On

In **Philippians 4:8**, we're encouraged, *"Finally, brothers and sisters, whatever is true, whatever is noble, whatever is right, whatever is pure, whatever is lovely, whatever is admirable—if anything is excellent or praiseworthy—think about such things."* This verse calls us to intentionally direct our thoughts toward what is good and uplifting.

Why Does It Matter to You?

Being positive matters because your mindset shapes your day. A positive attitude rooted in faith allows you to face challenges with hope, find joy in small blessings, and encourage those around you. It reflects your trust in God's plans, even when circumstances are tough.

Ask Yourself: *Am I focusing on the good things God is doing in my life, or am I letting negativity cloud my perspective?*

Call-to-Action: Choose positivity today by finding at least one blessing to celebrate, no matter how small. Speak words of encouragement to someone, and remind yourself of God's faithfulness in all things.

 Share this word with someone who inspires positivity in your life, and let's uplift one another with faith-filled attitudes.

Stay positive today—let your attitude reflect God's goodness and inspire hope in those around you.

80. TODAY'S WORD IS: COMPETENT

WEEK 12 DAY 3

Good morning!

Let's begin the day with a word that inspires confidence: **Competent.** Competence is not merely about meeting an unattainable standard of perfection; it revolves around possessing the crucial skills, deep insight, and abundant grace necessary to carry out your sacred duties effectively and purposefully. It ensures that you approach your assignments with the knowledge and understanding you need.

A Thought to Reflect On

2 Corinthians 3:5- 6 reminded us, *"Not that we are competent in ourselves to claim anything for ourselves, but our competence comes from God. He has made us competent as ministers of a new covenant—not of the letter but of the Spirit."* This verse teaches us that our abilities are empowered by God's Spirit, enabling us to serve His purpose faithfully.

Why Does It Matter to You?

Being competent matters because it gives you the confidence to embrace God's calling with faith and humility. Often, we face self-doubt, fearing we are not enough. But when you realize that your competence comes from God, it frees you from the pressure of relying solely on yourself.

Competence is also how you honor God. By using the skills, talents, and opportunities He has entrusted to you, you reflect His work in your life and inspire others to do the same. It's not about being the best but about being faithful to what He has given you and striving to serve Him well.

Ask Yourself: *Am I trusting in God's strength to make me competent, or am I letting self-doubt hold me back? How can I use my God-given abilities to glorify Him today?*

Call-to-Action: Identify a task or responsibility where you feel uncertain, and lean into God's promise to equip you. Step forward in faith, knowing He has given you what you need to fulfill His purpose.

🖋 **Share this word with someone who inspires you with their competence, and let's encourage one another to use our gifts for God's glory.**

Be confident in your competence today—God has equipped you to excel in the work He has called you to do.

81. TODAY'S WORD IS: SKILLFUL

WEEK 12 DAY 4

Good morning!

Let's begin the day with a word celebrating growth and excellence: **Skillful**. To be skillful is to develop and use the gifts God has given you, striving for mastery not for self-glory but to honor Him in all you do.

A Thought to Reflect On

In **Proverbs 22:29**, we're reminded, *"Do you see someone skilled in their work? They will serve before kings and not before officials of low rank."* This verse highlights the importance of honing and using our skills faithfully, knowing that excellence in our work brings opportunities to glorify God.

Why Does It Matter to You?

Being skillful matters because it reflects the care and effort you put into developing the gifts God has entrusted to you.

Skill is not just a natural ability—it results from dedication, learning, and perseverance.

When you grow in your skills, you can serve others more effectively, confidently meet challenges, and bring greater glory to God. Your pursuit of excellence can inspire those around you to do the same, creating a ripple effect of faithfulness and diligence.

Ask Yourself: *Am I using my skills to their full potential? How can I grow in skill and use it to serve God and others today?*

Call-to-Action: Take time today to focus on developing one skill, whether it's in your work, relationships, or spiritual life. Pray for wisdom and discipline, and dedicate your efforts to God's glory.

Share this word with someone who inspires you with their skillfulness, and let's encourage one another to strive for excellence in all we do.

Pursue skillfulness today—develop your gifts with care and dedication, honoring God through the work of your hands.

82. TODAY'S WORD IS: PRODUCTIVE

WEEK 12 DAY 5

Good morning!

Let's begin the day with a word that encourages intentional action: **Productive**. To be productive is to use your time, energy, and resources wisely, working with purpose to glorify God and bless others.

A Thought to Reflect On:

In **Colossians 3:23**, we're reminded, *"Whatever you do, work at it with all your heart, as working for the Lord, not for human masters."* This verse reminds us that productivity isn't about being busy—it's about working with excellence and purpose as an act of worship to God.

Why Does It Matter to You?

Being productive matters because your work and efforts reflect your faith and priorities. Productivity isn't about doing more—it's about doing what truly matters with focus and intention. It's about creating value in your life and the lives of others, knowing that every task, big or small, can bring glory to God.

Productivity also helps you steward the time and opportunities God has given you. By being intentional, you can achieve more, grow in your faith, and make a meaningful impact in the world around you.

Ask Yourself: *Am I using my time and energy wisely? How can I focus on what truly matters today?*

Call-to-Action: Identify one priority for the day where you can be intentionally productive. Dedicate your work to God, and let Him guide your actions to create value and impact.

📌 **Share this word with someone who inspires you with their productivity, and let's encourage one another to work with purpose and faith.**

Be productive today—focus on what matters, honor God with your efforts, and trust Him to bless the work of your hands.

83. TODAY'S WORD IS: RELIABLE

WEEK 12 DAY 6

Good morning!

Let's begin the day with a word that builds trust: **Reliable**. To be reliable is to be dependable and trustworthy, reflecting God's faithfulness in your actions and commitments.

A Thought to Reflect On

In **1 Corinthians 4:2**, we're reminded, *"Now it is required that those who have been given a trust must prove faithful."* This verse encourages us to be faithful stewards of the responsibilities and relationships God has entrusted to us, showing reliability in all that we do.

Why Does It Matter to You?

Being reliable matters because it strengthens relationships and reflects God's character. When people know they can count on you, it fosters trust, respect, and deeper connections. Your reliability is a testimony to your integrity and faithfulness, pointing others toward the consistency and faithfulness of God.

Reliability also teaches discipline and commitment. It challenges you to follow through on your word, honor your responsibilities, and be a source of stability for those around you.

Ask Yourself: *Am I someone others can rely on? How can I reflect God's faithfulness in my actions today?*

Call-to-Action: Identify one area where you can show greater reliability today—whether it's following through on a commitment, being present for someone, or completing a task with excellence. Let your actions reflect God's dependability and love.

Share this word with someone who inspires you with their reliability, and let's encourage one another to be faithful in all we do.

Be reliable today—honor your commitments, reflect God's faithfulness, and strengthen the trust others have in you.

84. WEEKLY PAUSE: NAVIGATING LIFE WITH FAITH AND RELIABILITY

Good morning!

This week, we reflected on being able, positive, productive, competent, skillful, and reliable. These words remind us that God equips us with the abilities, mindset, and faith to live purposefully and honor Him in all we do. Let's take this moment to pause and reflect on how these lessons have shaped our actions and attitudes this week.

Reflection

- Which word from this week resonated most deeply with you?
- How have you seen God working through your abilities, mindset, or actions to make an impact in your life and the lives of others?
- Are there areas where you feel God is calling you to grow in reliability or develop your skills further?

Check-In

- *What victories are you celebrating this week in using your gifts and abilities faithfully?*
- *What steps can you take to continue growing in competence, productivity, and reliability in the coming week?*

Prayer

Lord, thank You for equipping us with gifts, skills, and opportunities to serve You and others. Thank You for teaching us to be reliable, productive, and positive in all we do, reflecting Your faithfulness and love. Help us carry these lessons forward, grow in our abilities, and trust in Your guidance. May our lives continue to honor You in every word and deed. In Jesus' name, Amen.

Step confidently into the new week, using your God-given abilities to serve, grow, and reflect His glory.

85. TODAY'S WORD IS: BLESSINGS

WEEK 13 DAY 1

Good morning!

Let's begin the day with a word that invites us to recognize God's goodness: **Blessings**. Blessings are all around us—sometimes obvious, sometimes hidden, but always present as a reminder of God's love and faithfulness.

A Thought to Reflect On

In **Psalm 103:2**, we're reminded, *"Praise the Lord, my soul, and forget not all His benefits."* This verse encourages us to take a moment to reflect on God's blessings, big and small, and to offer Him praise for the many ways He provides for us.

Why Does It Matter to You?

Focusing on blessings matters because it shifts your perspective from what's lacking to what you have. It opens your heart to gratitude, deepens your faith, and reminds you of God's goodness in every season of life.

Blessings come in many forms—health, relationships, opportunities, and even lessons learned through challenges. When you take time to notice and appreciate them, you strengthen your connection to God and foster a spirit of contentment and joy.

Ask Yourself: *Am I mindful of the blessings God has placed in my life? How can I express my gratitude for them today?*

Call-to-Action: Take a moment to list three blessings in your life today, no matter how small. Offer a prayer of thanks to God, acknowledging His faithfulness and provision.

Share this word with someone who is a blessing in your life, and let's encourage each other to celebrate God's goodness.

Celebrate your blessings today—praise God for His faithfulness and let gratitude fill your heart.

86. TODAY'S WORD IS: GRATITUDE

WEEK 13 DAY 2

Good morning!

Let's begin the day with a word that transforms our perspective: **Gratitude**. Gratitude is the practice of acknowledging and giving thanks for the blessings in our lives, even when circumstances feel uncertain or challenging.

A Thought to Reflect On

In **Psalm 107:1**, we're reminded, *"Give thanks to the Lord, for He is good; His love endures forever."* This verse invites us to respond to God's goodness with a heart of gratitude, recognizing His enduring love and faithfulness.

Why Does It Matter to You?

Gratitude matters because it shifts your focus from what's missing to what's present. It reminds you of God's faithfulness, even in the smallest details of your life. Gratitude strengthens your faith, deepens your joy, and opens your heart to see God's hand in every situation.

Gratitude isn't just for the good times—it's a way to trust God in all circumstances, knowing that He is always working for your good.

Ask Yourself: *Am I practicing gratitude daily, or am I letting the worries of life overshadow the blessings?*

Call-to-Action: Take a moment today to thank God for something specific in your life. Whether it's a lesson learned, a prayer answered, or simply the gift of a new day, let gratitude guide your heart and actions.

Share this word with someone who inspires you to live with gratitude, and let's encourage one another to count our blessings.

Live with gratitude today—thank God for His goodness, and let a thankful heart transform your outlook on life.

87. TODAY'S WORD IS: THANKFULNESS

WEEK 13 DAY 3

Good morning!

Let's begin the day with a word that invites expression: **Thankfulness**. Thankfulness is more than acknowledging blessings—it's actively expressing your appreciation to God and others for the goodness in your life.

A Thought to Reflect On

In **1 Thessalonians 5:18**, we're reminded, *"Give thanks in all circumstances; for this is God's will for you in Christ Jesus."* This verse challenges us to maintain a spirit of thankfulness, even in difficult seasons, trusting that God is working all things for our good.

Why Does It Matter to You?

Thankfulness matters because it deepens your relationship with God and others. By expressing gratitude, you strengthen bonds, spread joy, and remind yourself of God's unwavering presence.

When you choose thankfulness, you practice faith—it's a declaration that you trust God's plans and recognize His blessings, no matter the circumstances.

Ask Yourself: *Am I actively showing my thankfulness to God and others, or do I take my blessings for granted?*

Call-to-Action: Today, thank someone who has blessed your life. Offer a prayer of thanks to God for His constant presence and provision.

Share this word with someone who inspires thankfulness in your life, and let's encourage one another to express gratitude freely.

Be thankful today—express your appreciation to God and those around you, and let thankfulness guide your heart and actions.

88. TODAY'S WORD IS: CONTENTMENT

WEEK 13 DAY 4

Good morning!

Let's begin the day with a word that brings peace: **Contentment**. Contentment is the quiet assurance that what you have is enough because God's provision is perfect, and His plans are always good.

A Thought to Reflect On

In **1 Timothy 6:6**, we're reminded, *"But godliness with contentment is great gain."* This verse highlights the spiritual strength found in being satisfied with God's blessings rather than chasing after more or comparing ourselves to others.

Why Does It Matter to You?

Contentment matters because it frees you from the constant desire for more and shifts your focus to God's sufficiency. It fosters gratitude, deepens faith, and brings peace, even in challenging circumstances.

When you embrace contentment, you reflect trust in God's plans and timing, knowing He will provide exactly what you need.

Ask Yourself: *Am I finding contentment in God's provision, or am I chasing after things that distract me from His purpose?*

Call-to-Action: Take time today to pause and thank God for what you have. Reflect on the ways He has provided for your needs, and choose to let contentment guide your heart and decisions.

Share this word with someone who inspires you to live with contentment, and let's encourage each other to find peace in God's provision.

Live contentedly today—trust God's provision, and let peace and gratitude fill your heart.

89. TODAY'S WORD IS: JOY

WEEK 13 DAY 5

Good morning!

Let's begin the day with a word that radiates gladness: **Joy**. Joy is not simply an emotion tied to circumstances —it's a deep, abiding sense of happiness that flows from knowing God and trusting in His goodness.

A Thought to Reflect On

In **Psalm 100:1-2**, we're reminded, *"Shout for joy to the Lord, all the earth. Worship the Lord with gladness; come before Him with joyful songs."* This verse invites us to celebrate God's goodness with hearts full of joy, reflecting His love and faithfulness in our lives.

Why Does It Matter to You?

Joy matters because it transcends fleeting happiness and brings lasting peace and hope. When you choose joy, you proclaim your trust in God's promises, even amid trials. Joy doesn't deny difficulties—it declares that God's love is greater than any challenge.

Joy is also contagious. Living with joy inspires others to see God's goodness and draw closer to Him. Ask yourself: *Am I living with joy that reflects my faith in God, or am I allowing circumstances to rob me of His gift of joy?*

Call-to-Action: Celebrate joy today by intentionally finding reasons to rejoice—whether it's through worship, laughter, or acts of kindness. Let your joy reflect the love and faithfulness of God.

🕊 **Share this word with someone who brings joy to your life, and let's encourage one another to celebrate God's goodness together.**

Rejoice today—let your joy reflect God's love, and share it with those around you.

90. TODAY'S WORD IS: REFLECTION

Good morning!

Let's begin the day with a word that invites stillness: **Reflection**. Reflection is the practice of looking back to see God's hand in your life, learning from the journey, and giving thanks for His faithfulness.

A Thought to Reflect On

In **1 Chronicles 16:12**, we're reminded, *"Remember the wonders He has done, His miracles and the judgments He pronounced."* This verse encourages us to pause and reflect on God's work in our lives—His blessings, guidance, and love that have carried us through every moment.

Why Does It Matter to You?

Reflection matters because it strengthens your faith by reminding you of God's past faithfulness. When you take time to look back, you can see how He has provided, answered prayers, and guided you through challenges. Reflection fosters gratitude and gives you confidence in His plans for the future.

Ask Yourself: *Am I taking the time to reflect on God's goodness, or am I rushing ahead without pausing to acknowledge His work in my life?*

Call-to-Action: Spend time today reflecting on the past quarter—consider the blessings, lessons, and growth you've experienced. Offer a prayer of gratitude for God's faithfulness and ask for His guidance as you move forward.

📌 **Share this word with someone who has been part of your journey, and let's encourage one another to reflect on God's goodness.**

Take time to reflect today—look back with gratitude, and let God's faithfulness inspire your next steps.

91. WEEKLY PAUSE: REFLECT ON YOUR BLESSINGS WITH GRATITUDE

WEEK 13 DAY 7

Good morning!

This week, we've focused on blessings, gratitude, thankfulness, contentment, joy, and reflection. These words remind us of the importance of pausing to acknowledge God's faithfulness, celebrating the blessings He has poured into our lives, and giving thanks for His presence in every moment.

Reflection

- What blessings are you most grateful for this quarter?
- How has focusing on gratitude deepened your faith and shifted your perspective?
- Are there areas in your life where God is calling you to express more thankfulness or joy?

Check-In

- *What victories are you celebrating this quarter?*
- *How can you carry a heart of gratitude into the next season of your life?*

Prayer

Lord, thank You for the countless blessings You have given us. Thank You for teaching us to live with gratitude, contentment, and joy, even in challenging moments. As we reflect on this quarter, we are reminded of Your faithfulness and love. Help us to carry these lessons forward, always acknowledging Your goodness and sharing it with others. In Jesus' name, Amen.

Step into the next quarter with gratitude, trusting in God's faithfulness, and celebrating His blessings in every season.

QUARTERLY REFLECTION
TYING IT ALL TOGETHER

As we close this quarter, let's take a moment to reflect on the journey we've walked together. Through words of faith, strength, growth, and gratitude, we've explored what it means to trust God, persevere through challenges, and celebrate His blessings in every season. This is our chance to pause, give thanks, and carry these lessons into the next chapter of life.

Quarterly Summary

This quarter, we've been reminded of:

• **God's Strength in Our Weakness**: Words like *hope, perseverance,* and *courage* encouraged us to face life's challenges with faith and resilience, trusting in God's unending power.

• **The Beauty of Growth and Change**: Through words like *transformation, adaptability,* and *flexibility,* we learned to embrace the changes God brings into our lives, knowing He uses them to shape us for His purpose.

• **The Power of Gratitude**: With words like *blessings, contentment,* and *joy,* we were reminded to pause and recognize God's faithfulness in both the big moments and the small details of life.

Each word built upon the next, creating a foundation of faith, hope, and purpose.

Reflection Questions

• Which word or theme from this quarter spoke most deeply to your heart?

• How have you grown spiritually, emotionally, or relationally through the lessons of this quarter?

• In what ways can you carry these lessons into the next chapter of your journey?

Encouragement for the Future

As we step into a new quarter, let's carry forward the truths we've learned. Life's journey is ever-changing, but God's faithfulness remains constant. Keep trusting, growing, and leaning into His plans for you.

Prayer

Lord, thank You for the journey of this quarter. Thank You for the lessons, the growth, and the reminders of Your faithfulness. As we reflect on this season, we are grateful for Your guidance and love that carried us through every moment. Help us to carry these truths into the next quarter with confidence, courage, and a heart fixed on You. May our lives continue to honor You in all we do. In Jesus' name, Amen.

A Note from the Author

Hi,

Congratulations on completing Volume 1 of the Word of the Day series! I am deeply grateful that you allowed me to be a part of your journey over the past quarter. Together, we have explored powerful words that have challenged, inspired, and encouraged us to grow in faith, resilience, and purpose.

This series was created to help you build a daily rhythm of reflection, scripture, and action, one word at a time. I pray that this first volume has empowered you to live more intentionally, strengthened your connection with God, and enriched your relationships with others.

As you reflect on the lessons and blessings of this quarter, consider revisiting the words that resonated most with you. Let them continue to shape and guide your journey. And don't keep the experience to yourself—share this volume with friends, family, or loved ones. Imagine the conversations and growth that could come from exploring these words together!

Looking Ahead

This is just the beginning! Each volume in the Word of the Day series is designed to build on the last, offering new words, scriptures, and insights to carry you through the seasons of life. Volume 2 is on the way, and I'm excited to continue this journey with you.

Thank you for allowing me to walk with you through this first quarter. It has been an honor to share these words and reflections with you. I pray that you carry these lessons into the next season, trusting God to guide your steps and grow your faith.

With gratitude,

Dr. Aigbefo D. Ehihi

About the Author

Dr. Aigbefo D. Ehihi is an ordained pastor, military chaplain, and bestselling author dedicated to inspiring faith, personal growth, and holistic living. With expertise in theology, leadership, and counseling, he combines spiritual wisdom with practical guidance to empower individuals to thrive.

As the author of *So Many Friends, So Little Friendship, Living Every Day with the Cross,* and *Hold Fast,* Dr. Ehihi inspires transformation through messages of grace, truth, and unwavering purpose. His heartfelt mission is to guide others toward greater heights through faith and God's Word.

ALSO BY AIGBEFO D. EHIHI

Dr. Aigbefo D. Ehihi's works are known for their profound insights, practical wisdom, and inspiring messages that empower readers to live with purpose, faith, and grace. Explore his other books:

- ***So Many Friends, So Little Friendship*** – A compelling look at the meaning of true friendship and how to nurture deeper, more authentic relationships.

- ***Living Every Day with the Cross*** – A transformative guide to embracing faith, grace, and God's purpose in your daily life.

- ***Hold Fast*** – A powerful call to resilience, perseverance, and unwavering trust in God during life's storms.

- ***The Silent Chapter****: Healing and Overcoming Your Silent Struggles* – An encouraging resource for confronting inner struggles and embracing healing and wholeness.

- ***PMCS: Preventive Maintenance for Couples Success*** – A practical guide for military couples, offering tools to strengthen and sustain thriving relationships.

These works reflect Dr. Ehihi's mission to uplift and inspire others through faith and personal growth.

Discover more at www.aishific.com and embark on a journey of transformation today.